W9-BOK-560

The Beard and I

The Beard and I

by

TOMMY WHITEHEAD

DAVID McKAY COMPANY, INC.

New York

THE BEARD AND I

LIBRARY OF CONGRESS CATALOG CARD NUMBER: 65-20932

MANUFACTURED IN THE UNITED STATES OF AMERICA

VAN REES PRESS   •   NEW YORK

To My Absent Family

The Beard and I

CHAPTER 1

TWELVE years ago, in England, I was in a very pleasant groove. I had a son, then four years old, who, having taken eight years to produce, was still the apple of my eye and, living within chimney-pot view across the roofs of Kensington in London, I had a lovely young daughter, married to a charming and handsome young man. They had produced, on my birthday, a little girl—my granddaughter Sarah, whom I adored.

I was a young (and even younger looking, so I was told) grandmother. My husband was handsome, energetic, and doing well. The war was over and we had a small Town house which we had just fixed the way we wanted. We sailed at weekends at Chichester Harbor, where we had a minute cottage. In the winter we beagled and walked and sawed wood for the fires. We were happy—because we were building up our lives again.

Alas, how short a time this state of bliss was to last. A small cloud appeared on the horizon one day when my husband came home and said he had to go to America and then on round the world on business. It was impossible that I should go too because in England at that stage money could not be used for foreign travel. I was sad and mad.

America, to me, was Shrangri-la. I had always had a "thing" about Americans: we had had many friends in the American Navy during the war; it was the *only* country I wanted to visit. It was very hard to accept the prospect of being alone, or rather husbandless, for four months—the length of the proposed visit.

However, off he went. This, surely, is the greatest contri-

1

bution made to shareholders in an expanding business—this sacrifice made by the wife and mother of a family in allowing herself to be left in the groove alone.

In view of what I have experienced since my husband departed for the United States for the first time, I am amazed that the powers that be can be so short-sighted as to not allow wives to go along with their husbands on business trips of any length. I know that the mothers of young children would often find it difficult to leave them, but the psychological difference between staying at home because one doesn't want to leave one's babies and staying because one just can't afford to go, is enormous.

Here I was, once again husbandless. Life was *all right*, you know, but it lacked spark. Everything went on as before. My daughter Jacqueline and her husband joined me every weekend at our cottage, but it was all so different. I had to get things ready on Friday evenings for the weekend, pack them in the car, lift my sleeping son in his little sleeping bag and install him on the back seat, drive the car for seventy miles, get out, open a gate, drive the car through, get out, shut the gate, repeat this performance in a field where cows were grazing (animals which are, to me, almost as terrifying as mice), drive through a dark wood to the little cottage that stood alone in a small clearing surrounded by trees which at night creaked ominously, find the hidden key of the cottage in a dark corner where untold wettish things lurked, let myself in, get the lights on and the heaters going, put hot water bottles in the beds, lift my son into his bed, unpack the car, put the food away, look into the bathroom and discover several large spiders with fat legs lying in wait, and finally to rush frantically up the stairs to bed—alone. That was the hell of it—*alone!*

Of course in the morning things were different. The family would arrive and the close proximity to nature, the bird calls, the wanderings through the woods while drinking one's

2

morning tea, were as blissful as ever. This was still the loveliest place we could think of. On Sunday nights the Friday night procedure reversed itself, although this time my darling son-in-law, Keith, would do his best to relieve me of all the horrid tasks.

To digress—Keith is a young man who, being a naturalist, has always somehow met women who regarded such things as field mice nesting in the sofa as rather sweet. And it is to his eternal credit that he didn't immediately hate me when he discovered that I was not happy with that sort of thing.

Keith would walk along the sea wall, binoculars at the ready. Even without them, he could identify tiny birds at tremendous distances. He would study the sky and the sea, then go home and paint a wonderful picture. Alas, the naturalist in him caused him to be interested in what were to me rather gruesome objects. It was with no surprise, and certainly with no pleasure, that I found him examining a very dead bird that looked like a large gull. On the kitchen table.

"This is very interesting," said he. "It's an unusual bird for these parts." "But it's disgusting," I said. The decomposing bird was deposited out-of-doors. For the rest of the day Keith was to be found peering at it, or looking up things in reference books, and the whole evening he brooded over the odd shape of its beak. The next day, I was away from the cottage for some time, and on my return I went into the kitchen, to make some tea no doubt. There was a small saucepan on the stove—filled with water which was boiling like mad and spluttering away. There was a sticklike thing protruding from the top of the saucepan. A most unappetizing odor filled the kitchen. How odd, I thought. Keith must be boiling his brushes. I turned the gas down lower, grasped the sticklike thing to see what was happening, and pulled out of the saucepan the horrid head of the bird. I was holding the beak. I *thought* it hadn't smelled like paint. I dropped the thing, uttering a primeval cry. Keith explained

3

that he had to get the flesh and feathers off because he wanted to draw the skull and then take it to the British Museum.

Having made certain that the saucepan was disposed of so that we could never again use it for cooking, I examined the bare bones of the bird. Far more attractive now, I had to admit, than it had been when adorned with decayed feathers.

Keith was right of course. It was an unusual bird for those parts. It was confirmed by the British Museum, where it now reposes, that it was *Colymbus adamsii* (loon, to Americans), the white-billed northern diver, American variety, with only two previous authenticated records in Britain. The last one in 1880.

It was interesting, but to my mind a poor exchange for my migrating businessman, last observed on those shores four months before.

I was living the life of many American women: husbandless, responsible for all the day-to-day problems that inevitably occur once one has possessions.

The roof leaked in the London house; it had snowed and, as the snow melted, the water had forced itself between the slates and through the ceiling of my son's room, where it hung suspended in a big belly made by the recently carefully selected wallpaper. An umbrella prodded into the lowest point of the large bulge produced a stream which just missed the flower vase placed below in anticipation. The snow had to be got off the roof. It was after five o'clock (when the British workman lays down his tools), so someone had to get up there. *I.* After indescribable struggles with ladders suspended over stairwells, horrid moments of vertigo when I looked down, loud cries to my son to "move off the ladder darling in case Mummy falls off," I finally found myself standing on the roof of 44 Kensington Place, late in the evening, with the sun slowly disappearing in the West. The West: America; that's where he was, and I was shoveling

4

snow off the roof of *his* house to save *his* carpets and *his* furniture.

During this period we had received many letters describing the trip. Of course one was interested. One loved this fellow who was now staying at the Beverly Hills Hotel. But all the same one was just faintly annoyed. Every letter told us how much he missed us; we knew that he loved us too; but when one got letters from American people he had met telling us how much they had enjoyed meeting our husband and enclosing photographs—gorgeous, of course, and with a swimming pool in the background—we became positively cross. In spite of the fact that they always said they were most anxious to meet us, and our husband was "just darling."

Finally, years later, the four-month trip ended and the moment we saw him all the swimming pools, and the rather unnerving glamor, became unimportant.

Twelve years ago postwar rationing still existed in England and one of the presents Edward brought back from the Land of Plenty was a parcel of steaks packed in dry ice.

This was terrific. Steaks had been unprocurable, except at one place in Plymouth where, during the war, one could always get a steak. It was after I had eaten several of these —over a period of months, of course—that the restaurateur was arrested for serving horsemeat to his customers without acquainting them with that fact.

However, here we were with six juicy steaks—guaranteed nonhorse. We telephoned my daughter and son-in-law and invited them to dinner. Two good bottles of wine were opened; potatoes were put in the oven to bake; a green salad was tossed in what we were now told by our husband was the American fashion (although we had always done it that way), and here I was, prepared to grill the steaks.

This is one great difference between our countries. *I* was going to grill the steaks and my husband was going to allow me to. One thing we had not thought of—the grill. We had read American magazines and we had heard of barbecues. Indeed, at our cottage we always cooked things that smelled strongly, out of doors on an iron grill over a wood fire, but we had never thought of that as barbecuing. We did it for two reasons: one, because we didn't like the smell of things burning inside the cottage (and we were always being shown wonders of nature by our son, just as we began getting the meal, which caused me to forget things on the stove), and two, we adored the lovely crisp outside of the meat or fish when it had been cooked this way. But it wasn't barbecuing to us; it was just cooking outside.

Anyway, here we are once again back in London. Twelve years ago, with six steaks to cook. We were told by our recently returned expert on American cooking that the steaks had to be broiled. This brought about our first misunderstanding. To broil meat in England—a fate to which only the less glamorous cuts of meat are subjected—one melts butter in a large casserole, fries the meat on both sides until it is brown, adds a few large whole onions, then carrots, and then a couple of inches of water. The lid of the casserole is put on firmly and the concoction is placed in a very slow oven or on a low flame on top of the stove. If one remembers to look at it before the whole thing becomes a blackened mess that is impossible to get off, it is delicious, but I could not believe that Edward wanted me to do this with his beautiful American steaks which had flown the Atlantic First Class. I was right, he hadn't been thinking of broiling English, but broiling American, which is grilling English, which as everyone knows is done by applying heat from above in an open oven.

At that time the cooker, as we called it, in a small household in England had a tiny grill crouching underneath the burners, which would just about toast four small bits of bread for breakfast if one got up early and got the grill hot and then stood over the bits of bread doing a sort of square dance with them.

6

This, sad to say, was the fate of the steaks. There they reposed, looking like an advertisement in the *Ladies Home Journal* one minute, and then they were being chased round two at a time. Problem: how to keep the others hot without overcooking them? This was another thing: I was told by my expert that Americans just didn't eat overdone meat. . . .

At last they were carried into the dining room, garnished with mushrooms and onions. The salad was served and the wine was poured when my system, crushed by the battle I had endured and my efforts to live up to the ideal American Woman (and also with faint memories of the horse dealer in Plymouth), revolted.

As I picked up my knife and fork and leaned forward to attack my prime cut steak, enough under rationing to feed a person for a week, my head suddenly reeled. My plate seemed to swim toward me. To my unaccustomed eye there was far too much animal about this meal. Feebly waving away my concerned family, I climbed the thirty-three steps to my bedroom and lay in the darkness listening to a stampeding herd of beef on the hoof drum across my pillow. And downstairs my abandoned steak, my beautiful Texas steak, was gobbled up by Willie, our gourmet dog, who had never tasted steak before and who thereafter refused to eat his previously favorite and perfectly scrumptious combination of asparagus and chopped-up whale meat.

CHAPTER 2

TO REACH our happy state of twelve years ago, Edward and I had lived more than half our alloted span, Edward appropriately ahead of me on the downward path.

We had left our homes—mine in Wales and Edward's in Hampshire, England—while we were in our teens. I, after an overprotected early youth, in my mid-teens—I just couldn't *wait*—and Edward in his late teens, so that we converged on London seeking independence at about the same time, historically speaking.

Independence is undoubtedly *the* thing to acquire and nothing has ever been quite so satisfying as the dress bought with one's own earned money, the meal eaten in one's own bed-sitter with a book propped up against one's own potted plant. All paid for by oneself! Bliss!

We were teenagers, but we were not called that then. Teenagers had not been invented in the way that they exist today and although London was full of young people doing jobs there was none of this organized lawlessness that takes place on both sides of the Atlantic now. Naturally, I have a theory about this. I think that young people still living in their parents' homes, never having to consider where the next boiled egg is coming from, never having to wonder if their shirts will be back from the laundry, never having to face the fact that the landlady's smile will rapidly disappear if the rent isn't paid, never having to rely on getting themselves out of bed in the morning, never having, in fact, any responsibility, are not only deprived but are so darned bored that they are bound to look for trouble. So I think that parents are much to blame for not kicking out their children if they don't show signs themselves of wanting to go. And the poor are even worse than the rich. Poor old Mum gets her greatest pleasure from attending to the wants of a great youth grown much too large for the nest, showering attentions on him that poor old Dad would love to share. How, if these enormous late-teenagers are always cluttering up their lives are Mum and Dad ever going to work out a decent sort of relationship with each other? The young who do leave home experience homesickness and loneliness of course, but without ever having felt lonely or sad how can one grow into a complete adult?

Once one has got over the initial wrench, the bliss of being able to get home late without feeling that someone has been straining her ears since nine-thirty listening for one's return is unbelievable. Landladies can be boring in this way too, but one did not feel one was breaking a landlady's heart if one wasn't home before ten-thirty.

In theory the landlady of the house where I lived near Lancaster Gate in London was a sort of chaperone, but my recollection is that she only took her duties seriously after eleven P.M. In the landlady's world, one felt, sex only happened after this hour—anyway she was apt to lurk in hallways at about 11:30 just in case a jolly evening at the cinema had let down one's defenses sufficiently to induce one to invite one's young man up to one's room for an orgy. Before 11 P.M. troops of young men would be allowed in, usually those one had been avoiding for weeks, and I doubt whether the landlady would have stirred from her wireless if above the strains of Al Bowley singing "Night and Day" she had heard sounds of a maiden in ecstasy—which she didn't from my room. I wasn't much given to making a lot of noise.

My first job had been in an hotel in Kensington, where I did the flowers, sat at the reception desk, sometimes helped the housekeeper sort out linen in a huge room with a glass dome at the top of the building—a job I loved. I also looked after the hotel kittens, once had the Manageress' puppy to sleep with me—disapproved of by my landlady and also much re-

9

gretted by me in the morning—and fought off the attentions of the owner of the hotel who was terribly old—about forty.

I was spared the necessity of giving up my job to avoid the persistent old gent by being offered another one.

A very old-established firm of woolen merchants were about to burst into the field of ladies' dresses and bathing suits under the trade name of "Femina." They were looking for a girl to work in the designs room who could also feature in their advertisements. Preferably a girl whose face had not appeared in an advertisement before. This was exactly right for me. There was the undoubted glamor attached to being a model and also I could use what creative ability I possessed.

This job grew and grew with time and it continued through the tragedy of a fiancé crashing to his death in an airplane while rehearsing for the Royal Air Force flying display at Hendon, and through a subsequent rebound marriage. A marriage which was bound to fail and which quickly did, but which resulted in a small daughter. Jacqueline. A beautiful calm child who more than made up for the miserable two years that preceded her birth.

Edward had left his home in Hampshire and lived in Kensington, London, about one mile from where I had my first digs. He shared a flat with other young men and lived on a grander scale than I had in my early days. Young men are generally so clever about their living arrangements. They make an effort to find, and preserve, obliging old bodies who will do for them, whereas girls usually prefer to do for themselves and spend the cash saved on clothes.

When I began my independent life it was sometimes suggested that I share a flat with another girl or girls, but one glance at a bedroom littered with crumpled clothes, or a bathroom with laundry dripping on one's head, or a kitchen with a comb full of hairs on the draining board and I would creep happily back to my one-room paradise.

Edward lived a pretty social life. Then, as now, mothers of daughters who were "coming out"—being Presented at Court in those days—and doing the London season had problems with young men. Not problems of fighting them off but problems of getting enough of them to go to the dances they were giving for their daughters. Once a young man appeared at a dance, especially if he happened to be good-looking and had decent manners, he was "on the list" and if he wished he could dine out every night and dance till dawn. All he needed was a large supply of boiled shirts—or friends the same size—and stamina. In those days the shirts gave out first. In return he would take a pretty girl to the theater, or to lunch in the country on a Sunday. The young man with a conscience would give a cocktail party and invite the people who had invited him, but many young men accepted invitations to Ascot or Goodwood or Cowes and never made any attempt to return hospitality. Still they were asked! How foolish can a fond mother—or father—get?

Most young men would do at least one season this way but for Edward and his friends it soon palled and they sought more satisfying ways of spending their time. They sailed, they swam, they played squash, they hunted, they walked, they kept fit—cold baths in the morning and a brisk walk through the Park to their offices. They read Marcus Aurelius and discussed the merits of pacifism though they were all joining the reserves of the fighting Services in preparation for Hitler's war. They took gliding lessons, tuned up their cars, went to lectures on everything. They were busy with their jobs all day and busy living their personal lives in the evenings and at weekends. They went to the "Proms," to the Albert Hall to hear good music, and at home they also listened to jazz— Fats Waller, an old Edward favorite—he was alive then. And a mile away I was also listening to the Quintette of the Hot Club de France with Django Rheinhart playing his guitar— he was alive too. Edward and I swam in the same ocean but in different streams. We met some of the same people, but never each other. We swam and swam, round and round, and then one evening in November I went skating.

Queen's Ice Club was the chic place to go on Tuesday nights at that time. I went with a small group, unable to skate but game to try. I hired skates, wobbled out to my friends, stood clutching the rail for a moment, and there was Edward. Skating round he was, doing long slow strokes and with his arm around the waist of some wretched girl. Well, I was there to skate! I had my lesson. I was towed round the ice. I was picked up and set on my feet a dozen times by assorted males. But I was gaining courage. I made a wild dash to the center of the rink. For one moment I felt myself swoop like a swallow, then I crashed. Hard! When the mists cleared Edward's face was hovering over me in a cloud of little shooting stars and meteors. He helped me to my feet. "You have a lot of courage," quoth he, "but you do need more instruction. Would you come round with me?" We didn't talk. When we left the ice our respective partners were standing there looking rather gloomy. At the end of the session we were swept out of different doors and that, I thought, was that. But it wasn't!

On New Year's Eve *the* event in London was the Chelsea Arts Ball—a costume ball that took place at the Albert Hall. Two huge and very loud bands played at either end of the Hall; the tiered boxes contained parties of people drinking champagne. Supper was served on the top floor.

There were hundreds of people milling about, and more hundreds swaying about on the dance floor. As the evening progressed a few exhausted couples collapsed in the middle of the floor where they sat back to back, holding each other up. They were joined by others until eventually the remaining really hardy dancers had to maneuver through all the bodies.

The young man I went with was not in costume, so neither was I, but the rule was that unless one wore fancy dress one had to wear a mask. My young man—his name long forgotten —was the proud possessor of an opera cloak, which he wore over his tails for good measure. I rather fancied myself in a green satin mask and a delicious white dress à la Carole Lombard. This was the period of the slinky crepe dress cut on the bias, than which there has never been anything more seductive. We danced merrily until supper time.

We climbed the stairs to the top floor, sat ourselves down at a table with a group of newly acquired chums. I looked around me and there was Edward again, sitting at the next table with the same wretched girl. He was eyeing me, but without recognition. I removed my mask. We both got up, tottered down the stairs clutching each other, and danced until 5 A.M. That was when my escort caught up with us. As we were dragged apart I realized that we still knew nothing about each other except that he was Teddy and I was Tommy. So that again was that. But again it wasn't. In February my office phone rang. An unfamiliar voice which I recognized at once said "Tommy?"

Edward, incarcerated in his flat by a riding accident, had gone laboriously through the Business Directory asking every dress house if a girl called Tommy worked there. And that really *was* that.

We couldn't marry at once. A. P. Herbert, who had just published his book, *Holy Deadlock,* was battling with the powers that be to change the divorce laws of England. The only grounds for divorce was adultery. Any discussion with one's marriage partner was called collusion and in the eyes of the law this was a far worse crime than adultery. Needless to say, everyone who wanted a divorce had to collude like mad —very few divorces can have happened without some discussion between the opposing parties—and I and my partner in my very brief marriage were no exception. It made no difference though. One still had to wait months and months—even years and years—to be free. But this wasn't entirely a bad thing. After one hasty marriage I was not anxious to leap into the fray again without time to make certain that the next attempt would be more successful, and Edward, although he knew from the beginning that his fate was sealed, was not the impetuous type and was glad to have time to make absolutely certain that this was absolutely it.

We certainly had time. Three years of various kinds of frustration followed but they were not wasted. I, and the small Jacqueline also, were put through a sort of training course.

Edward had thought far too deeply about what constituted the good life to change his habits just because he had fallen in love.

As a youth he had battled with a domineering parent for his independence. His father was crippled by rheumatoid arthritis and Edward remembers him as a difficult man who at the end of his life was totally incapacitated. Edward now realizes that the bad temper was undoubtedly caused by frustration and pain.

In Edward's teens he also began to suffer the pangs of arthritis. The conventional doctors he consulted muttered dark things about heredity and predisposition, but there was one doctor who visited his father who, on being told that the son of the house was apparently doomed to go the same way as his father, asked Edward to go and see him privately. Edward was told that the only way to cope with this awful looming future was to go on a strict diet. To cut out meat and starches, to eat only fresh fruit and salads, and to take lots of exercise in the open air.

As this was happening at Christmas time when the family sat down to roast turkey with all the trimmings and plum pudding served with rum butter, it took an awful lot of will power to refuse to eat anything but a salad with perhaps a nut and date to follow. Edward's poor mother was almost in tears, convinced that her only son was going to starve before her eyes, while his father was absolutely livid. Probably because the poor fellow, having spent large sums of money on every known cure, including literally and quite horrifyingly having gold injected into his veins by a doctor in Germany, could not bear to think that the possibility of salvation might

14

be in his own ability to resist the fleshpots. In the conventional fashion the father refused to believe that any man could "keep up his strength" without "good food," good food being steak and kidney pies, bacon and eggs, the roast beef of old England followed by pies and puddings—all first-class nourishers of arthritis.

The fact that Edward preferred to believe in the simple remedy and had the strength of mind to put it into practice must have made him an incompatible companion for a man who rejected the idea that the food he ate had any bearing on the disease he suffered, so, as Edward was by this time working for an insurance company in London, he took up his abode in the metropolis, where I was lurking, waiting to be saved.

By the time Edward and I met he was a very fit young man whose social life was by no means impaired by his unconventional attitude toward food. Indeed, his capacity to withstand the rigors of a social life in London was even greater than it would otherwise have been.

My training had to be got under way, and the first thing I had to be taught was to breathe, so that I could at least keep within hailing distance when taken for a walk. Since leaving the wilds of Wales, where naturally I had walked if I wanted to go anywhere, exercise for me had consisted of doing the night club shuffle—an almost motionless dance step—at the "400," where the atmosphere made deep breathing extremely hazardous, so I wasn't exactly in racing trim. But I was determined not to be left at the post.

Everyone I had known previously had planted me in a grandstand while they played rugger or in a deck chair for cricket, but not so Edward. He disliked team games; the periods of inactivity that must occur while someone else rushes about with a ball would bore him. When getting his exercise, he must be in motion all the time so I walked and walked and one of the things I discovered was that Edward had a tremendous love of the countryside, a positive passion —which he still has—and which he wanted to share with me.

15

Not for him the beaten path where one might meet hikers. He would strike off across country, over hill and dale, crossing small rivers, through beech woods and bluebell woods, through small gaps in hedges, and somehow, with Edward, something always happened. A foal would be born in a field, or a calf. Newly born lambs would be bleating in a fold, a hare would get up at our feet, he would know where to find primroses and meadow sweet; he'd stand breathing in great gulps of scented air, and I, following suit, found my own lungs expanding for the first time in years.

At the end of a walk he'd know just the right farmhouse where we could have tea in the parlor, with the farmer's wife boiling us eggs exactly the way we wanted them. Brown eggs in blue egg cups. How could one not have confidence in a young man who achieved such things?

Teddy's usual Sunday recreation was riding. He rode an Arab horse called Sorbo which positively bounced along, rolling red eyes and arching his neck. I had been inspired with so much confidence in my own physical abilities by Edward that I even agreed to ride with him, though I insisted that I have the quietest horse available when I made my effort.

One wonders if one's bravery is appreciated when one leaps into cold dark water, or walks along a narrow path with a precipice on one side, or, as in this case, when one agrees to mount a creature ten feet high. A creature armed with four iron-shod feet which stamp around continuously and a huge mouth full of long yellow teeth.

Edward did not really understand my fears or appreciate my bravery. He is an excellent horseman and of all creatures horses are his favorite. I had got the message and was willing to learn to care—but not very willing.

As we drove out of London one November morning the city was enveloped in a yellow fog. I prayed that the fog would extend as far as the stables we were bound for, but I was not to be spared. The sun came out as we approached and there, standing in the stable yard, was a dejected-looking animal. Even I, with my inborn terror of horses, thought he looked sad. His neck drooped toward the ground, so did his ears. He had long eyelashes, which also drooped, and lips which hung down loosely in a relaxed pout. His knees were bent and he had the roundest stomach—full of wind, it transpired—and the hollowest back imaginable. Pippin, this noble creature was called.

As I was helped into the saddle I found myself wondering how he could possibly carry me. Pippin had one little idiosyncrasy, we were told. He bit the behinds of horses in front of him if they were foolish enough to stay there, so when we set off I had to lead the way, with Teddy giving me instructions from the rear. We had to ride up a steep hill to reach the Hog's Back, which is a long ridge covered with springy turf. I found it extremely difficult to sit on a horse that sloped backward at a steep angle and when Pippin, as he exerted himself to climb, began to emit some of the wind of which he was so largely composed into the face of Edward's well-bred horse, I was not only frightened but also embarrassed. One was very inhibited in those days.

When we got to the top, Pippin grazed happily with me sliding down his neck. He even wandered into somebody's garden and began eating the flowers. Teddy had to take my reins and pull us out with the reluctant Pippin's neck stretched out yards. He was not a very responsive horse and the only time he showed any interest was when Teddy tried to ride ahead. He would give a quick lunge with his teeth, disturbing my equilibrium so that I had to plead with Teddy to stay alongside. We ambled slowly along and finally he said we'd better return to the stables. As we turned our horses' heads Edward began telling me how to rise to the trot if my steed could ever be persuaded to get out of first gear, but there were no half measures with Pippin. The moment he realized he was pointing in the direction of lunch he gathered himself and charged off, hooves pounding, leather flying

17

—my feet had come out of the irons with his first bound—
and with me hanging onto handfuls of mane and trying hard
not to pull it out in case it made him madder. I heard Edward shout, "Grip with your knees," but my knees were jelly
so how could I? Anyway how can one grip with one's knees
a rocketing bag of muscle and bone four feet wide? Edward
was shouting instructions as he galloped along behind me,
his horse's head with its rolling red eye and gnashing teeth
within inches of my calf. On we thundered and although at
no time did I gain confidence, I did have time to wonder
how I looked from the rear and also if a future filled with
episodes such as this was exactly what I wanted. But when
Pippin finally and very suddenly stopped galloping, so that
Edward's horse had to swerve to avoid collision and Edward
said "You were terrific," I found myself mentally preparing
to meet the challenge again in any area he cared to suggest.

I never became a horsewoman, neither did I become a
long-distance walker nor a strong swimmer nor a hard-
weather sailor. In retrospect it is surprising that our relationship survived my many failures in the field of outdoor sports.

CHAPTER 3

EDWARD'S oldest and greatest friend, the man who influenced him most during his young manhood, was Dr. Edward Griffith, a well-known name in the world of psychological medicine in England and, more recently, in America too. He had been a medical practitioner in Edward's home town and they had met when Edward had to brake a speeding toboggan by sticking out his foot, thereby breaking his leg bones and necessitating a long stay at the local hospital where "G," as he is known to his friends, attended him. G, about fourteen years older than Edward, was just the kind of friend Teddy needed at the time. A deep-thinking, sometimes irascible, highly amusing, and always generous man who helped broaden Teddy's interests to include philosophical subjects, and filled the void caused by Teddy's unhappy relationship with his father. Friendship with an older man is most important in the development of a young man's mind and how fortunate Teddy was to meet G at the crucial period of his life when he was casting himself adrift from his home.

By the time I came on the scene, G and Edward had been friends for many years. G had abandoned his medical practice and was concentrating on psychology, particularly as applied to marriage difficulties and human relations—so my horizons were widened too. For the first time I heard sex and all its associated problems discussed by intelligent people as calmly as most people discuss the weather. A tiny shock at first to my mind, which had labored under the delusion that sex had to be terribly secret and that everyone was self-taught! I was certainly not unusual in thinking this, G being one of the first doctors in England to write about sexual matters and to give lectures to mixed audiences on the subject.

I know Edward and I were helped through our waiting and testing period by G. After nearly forty years he remains Edward's closest friend.

Another great friend, another older man who became a great friend of both of us, was Ernest Bircher, the nephew of Dr. Bircher Benner of Zurich, Switzerland, who had virtually discovered vitamins and the fact that they are destroyed by cooking.

Ernest and his wife and four children lived in a large old house in Richmond where Edward and Jacqueline and I often visited them. The fact that they lived on a completely vegetarian diet and were all bursting with health confirmed and strengthened Edward's convictions that he was on the right track so far as the proper treatment of disease was concerned, though of course there had been dozens of people in Edward's life who thought he was more than slightly mad to prefer simple food to, for instance, *Caneton rouennais à la presse*. He, and I too when I became educated, soon learned that it was a great mistake to try to convert anyone to one's own way of thinking in the matter of food. People feel more strongly about it than they do about religion. Anyway, some just refused to believe that food had anything to do with disease, whereas they would go berserk if their nasty little dogs were given the wrong thing—be it white sugar or white bread—two things which I had come to believe, and still do, to be the curses of civilization. This was demonstrated to us when we were staying with friends who were dog-happy and were always busily breeding more of the little horrors. They were mean-looking little dogs, which lay in wait behind chairs and nipped one's calves as one passed by, and I was not fond of them.

One day I had found some whole wheat bread in the kitchen and bore it into the dining room feeling as though I had struck a vein of gold. The seven-year-old son of the house had leaped upon it with glad cries, whereupon the dog-loving mother said, "Stop! You can't eat that!" "Why not?" asked I, "it is quite fresh." "But it belongs to the dogs." "Why," said I, "can't the dogs have the white bread?" "Because," she said, "if I feed them on white bread their teeth will drop out and they will lose the urge to breed." "And what about your son?" said I.

I was given to understand that it was different for people.

I expect those old dogs will continue breeding and biting the unsuspecting with their sharp little teeth—all their own —long after that small boy has spent his fortune on dentist's bills and sterility tests.

One cannot pretend that because we have these beliefs we have never had a day's illness, but we do believe that without our convictions and our efforts to live according to them the waters would have closed over our heads a long time ago.

Also, alas, what we believe in, while frightfully good for one physically, is apt to be a tiny bit of a bore socially, so we have had to compromise when away from home.

Anyway, to resume the Bircher saga. Ernest was and still is a terribly handsome man with the most beautiful speaking voice I have ever heard and it was a joy to dine at his house and discuss the futilities of existence and how to rise above them. He and his family were great sunbathers, as was Edward, and so in a smaller way were Jacq and I. However, the Birchers did not only believe in sunbathing, they believed in freeing the body of the fetters of clothing, so the children would rush about the house doing their exercises wearing the minimum.

After a winter of knowing the Birchers they told us they were going to have a holiday in the New Forest. Would Edward drive Jacq and me there to visit them? Yes, he would, so one beautiful summer's day we set out.

We arrived at the entrance gates of a large country house just before lunch time. The gates were closed—locked—and when we honked an old crone came out of the lodge, who scrutinized us and asked us who we were visiting before admitting us.

As we drove up the long driveway I had a sudden flash of intuition. "Heavens, Teddy," I croaked, "I think this must be a nudist camp." We were approaching the front door, which opened just as I had got to the point of persuading Teddy to drive away and telephone our friends to say we were sorry we couldn't make it.

Down the steps tripped the Birchers' Swiss maid, who had been waiting for us. Dressed, but only just. She was wearing slacks and a buttoned-up sweater, which strained across her large unbrassiered bosom, leaving little ovals of flesh visible all the way down the front. Obviously a quick cover-up job.

"Ah good, everyone waits," she cried as she unhooked my fingers one by one from the side of the car.

"What shall we *do*?" I asked Edward. "We can't go away now," said he. "We'll have to see the Birchers and tell them we can't stay."

"Promise me you won't take off your pants," I said—I was beginning to know Edward. I think he agreed but Edward swears he would not have committed himself on such a lovely day.

We were ushered into a large hall with doors facing us, which bore the notice, "Guests must be dressed in the main hall." My fears were confirmed. The maid opened the doors. I closed my eyes, but had to open them when I fell down a step and there, illuminated in a brilliant square of light, running towards us was the whole Bircher family. Starkers! Not one stitch was anyone wearing. I kept my eyes strictly at eye level while we exchanged greetings, and was led to a seat at a low table in the garden.

The four-year-old Jacqueline immediately removed the single tiny garment she had been wearing and romped away. Edward took off his shirt, which made me nervous, and I put on my sunglasses and folded my arms tightly over my cotton dress.

Safe behind my sunglasses, I surveyed the landscape. We were in a lovely garden surrounded by high hedges, which made it a complete sun trap. The sun shone down on groups of people lying on the grass reading or chatting. A little farther away was a small lake where a few people were swimming while others leaped about a badminton court. There were about fifty people in all. Children, young men and women, fathers and mothers, grandfathers and grandmothers. Strong, healthy-looking bodies, lovely children's bodies, hardly anyone fat, though some too thin, and some rather broken, but all with skin tanned to a lovely pale brown all over.

Within ten minutes no one looked naked to me. My reactions were being observed and the children began asking me why I didn't undress. "It's too cold," I said as the sun beat down on me. Edward had disappeared. I had no support. The Bircher parents now began importuning me. In the nicest possible way, of course, they implied that my attitude was quite wrong and anyway no one would even look at me. This I could not believe. I had been looked at with my clothes on— why should anyone not look when I was wearing nothing? I was beginning to feel a little ashamed of my narrow-mindedness but I would not give in. Then I spotted Teddy. Playing badminton he was. A foursome, and as naked as the day he'd been born. I don't say I immediately rushed off and undressed, but I allowed myself to be persuaded next time it was suggested I should disrobe. I crept out of my dress and stood revealed in a three-piece suntan. Almost at once people, fascinating, intelligent people, drifted over to join our little circle. But I wasn't really relaxed. I decided to swim, so carrying Jacqueline, who was very surprised because I didn't usually carry her about, I walked to the lake closely followed by three gentlemen who were apparently anxious that I should not drown.

When Edward returned to the fold I was being photographed by a very distinguished-looking gentleman who wore nothing but a hearing aid, which peeved Edward somewhat—the camera, not the hearing aid—he hadn't thought I would lose my inhibitions so quickly. I chided him for letting me down and he said, "In the circumstances disrobing was the only way to make oneself inconspicuous."

We did not become ardent nudists. That was the only time we indulged but we did learn that nudist camps are utterly respectable. We feel one's daughter would be as safe in one as she wanted to be, though not necessarily as safe as one wanted her to be. I also learned never to be surprised by what might crop up with Edward.

The distinguished nudist amateur photographer turned out to be an American who, no doubt to placate Edward, said he would send him the snapshots. A package from New York arrived months later at Edward's club in London where he, absentmindedly opening it in the front hall while talking to some friends, had the misfortune to drop it, scattering the enlargements over the parquet.

It took some time to live down the rumor that he was trafficking in filthy pictures.

CHAPTER 4

THE months and years passed. Edward and I were living separate lives though we got together at weekends at the houses of friends and for sailing in the summer at a tiny cottage that Teddy had acquired at Bosham in Sussex.

It had been christened "Multum in Parva" by the wife of an Admiral who had previously owned it, but "Castle Beastly" is the name by which it has gone down in our history.

Bosham, which figures in the Bayeaux Tapestry, is one of the most attractive villages in England, with a lovely flint church well over a thousand years old in which is the tomb of the young daughter of King Canute. Henry V is supposed to have prayed in the church before setting sail for France and the Battle of Agincourt.

Almost all the houses date from the eighteenth century or earlier. The village green in front of the church is regularly flooded at "high water springs." In the ancient black tarred wooden buildings on the quay, where fishermen used to keep their nets, the wives of members of the Bosham Sailing Club served tea at weekends. There was and is about the place a somnolent charm that defies spoilation even in this day and age; largely because it lies at the head of a creek, part of Chichester Harbor, and offers no attractions to the masses in motor cars heading for the beaches that flank the mouth of the harbor some miles away.

Castle Beastly, while possessing no architectural merit, had its own charm. It sat in a field where a pink horse grazed. Its windows and doors folded back to expose a wide view of its own creek, where swans flew with creaking wings in the evenings.

The small house was always bursting at the seams. One of

the things Edward had probably not considered, but which he took in his stride, was the fact that a young woman with a small daughter is almost never alone. And in my case, not only was the small daughter always attached, but she also had to be provided with companions. Consequently our courtship, if one can call it that, was conducted in the midst of a gaggle of small girls—the gaggle getting more giggly as the girls got older.

There it was. There was never any doubt in our minds that we should be spending our lives together eventually, but my gosh, it was a long time acoming.

Edward was successful in his job. He was by now Assistant Secretary to the Pall Mall office of his Company and he was assured by his superiors that he was destined for one of the top jobs in the Company.

He always got on well with people—that was always evident in his business life—and his job provided him with the opportunity to meet all sorts of people, many of whom are still his friends. He was gentle with Jacq and me, but he was never diffident in his job. He always had complete confidence in himself, so he inspired confidence in others. He went to infinite trouble to help his friends when necessary. He *really* was—is—a kind and gentle man.

When war was declared in 1939 we began to think our personal affairs would never be settled, that we'd all be bombed in our (separate) beds and that would be the end of it all.

Edward had joined the Royal Naval Volunteer Reserve in 1937. When he appeared before the Selection Board he was beardless, but he did sport a flourishing moustache of which he was extremely proud.

At the conclusion of the interview a member of the Board remarked, "You realize, Whitehead, that if you join the Navy you'll have to lose that magnificent moustache?" "If that is all I shall lose, Sir, I'll have little cause for complaint," he replied.

On the first day of the war in September 1939, Edward and I were at Bosham. A day I shall always remember. It was gloriously sunny, so, having listened to Chamberlain's speech on the radio and experienced our first (false) air raid alarm, we decided to have a last sail in his sloop Dinah. Edward didn't shave that morning, because he knew he'd get his call-up papers soon and, although he had made his gallant speech to the RNVR selection board, he was not really anxious to lose his moustache. I should explain here that in the Royal Navy a moustache alone is taboo. One must have a "full set." All the hair on a man's face must be allowed to luxuriate—no shaving of the cheeks or the sides of the chin. It has to be all or nothing.

I had previously had a boy friend, a painter, who sported a beard, but it was black and curly and grew high up on his cheeks, so that he seemed to be peeping over a hedge. It also smelled of Lifebuoy soap, which made me suspect that he suspected that he might have B.O. Which was terribly off-putting. Poor fellow, he couldn't win.

The pattern of bristles on Edward's face grew in a pleasing design, and furthermore they appeared to be blonde. Apparently one never knows with whiskers; they sometimes come out a completely different color from the hair on the head.

Edward knew that once in the Navy he would not be allowed to grow a beard without seeking permission from his Commanding Officer and Commanding Officers had been known to refuse depending, one supposes, on the amount of topiary around already. But if a man arrived already whiskered and with all his identification photographs displaying it, he would not be asked to remove it, though he would still have to have permission to shave it off if he got tired of it, and that might be refused too.

So the race was on. Would the beard grow before the summons came? It did. Nourished by the late autumn sunshine, the golden hair grew like corn, and within two months when

Edward joined the Navy he had a quite dashing beard and the beautiful moustache was saved. The only further repercussion was that I developed a horrid rash on my cheeks, which disappeared as Edward's whiskers grew silky.

CHAPTER 5

EDWARD formally joined the Service as a sub-lieutenant. Following his preliminary training he was posted to H.M.S. "Impregnable," a stone frigate on Plymouth Sound, where raw recruits were changed into qualified signalmen in a period of six months. From the beginning Edward found that he was interested in the processes by which a young man, some not so young, from the industrial North could be so transformed, physically and mentally. He took a particular interest in physical training and in seamanship, carrying out his theory that the human mind works better in a healthy body. Parties of sailors would be taken by Edward to race in sailing cutters and whalers against other ships. Sailors who had never been in a sailing boat, or possibly any other kind of boat, would find themselves hauling on lines and hoisting sails, and in spite of the fact that most of them couldn't swim, and the sea in Plymouth Sound is hardly ever calm, they always clamored for more.

The boys who had sailed all day hardly ever had the energy to chase the local belles or create a disturbance during the evening. Another answer to the Mods and Rockers?

In Plymouth, at last, Edward and I began our married life. The processes of the law, helped along by A. P. Herbert, had been speeded up after the declaration of war, and on September 13, 1940 I was a free woman. On September 14, 1940 in London during a day-long air raid that was decisive in the Battle of Britain, Edward and I were married. We had a small party in the bomb shelter of a house on Park Lane belonging to our friend Dr. Dieter, in whose beautiful yacht "Terminist," a converted Brixham trawler, we used to sail before the war. He was one of the first Americans to join the RNVR and served for the duration in coastal forces. Eventually he became godfather to our son Charles.

Edward and I spent a very short night in a London hotel where we were the only people upstairs. As we entered the lift to go up to our room, droves of people clutching hot water bottles and rugs were arranging themselves in serried ranks on the floor of the foyer.

Early next morning we went to the country to fetch Jacqueline, and at last we could begin living, after marking time for three years.

Edward, with his usual good fortune, found us a heavenly small house on a large estate, which we rented furnished. It was on the banks of the River Yealm, a wide tidal river about four miles from Plymouth as the bomber flew, and there Jacqueline and I stayed for the duration of the war. For a while we were able to live as a family, though Edward of course lived on board when he was on duty, and he was on duty most of the time.

Plymouth, being a large naval port, received a great deal of attention from German bombers. We all spent many nights either listening to bombardments from our beds or, when the bangs seemed to be too close—as they often were when a German navigator mistook our finger of water for the one leading to the Naval Dockyard—from under the dining table, where we sometimes crouched with our pillows and blankets until the "all clear" sounded, when we would go outside to see whether a swan, which regularly nested twenty feet from our door, had survived. She always had.

The extraordinary thing about this period of our lives is that Jacqueline, who had to be wakened most nights, either to snuggle into my bed or for a session under the table, positively blossomed. Proving, I think, the importance of family feeling. Not only did she blossom, she grew to look like Edward: so much so that the village gossip was heard to say, "No matter what Mrs. Whitehead says I think she met the Lieutenant a long time before she says she did."

When Edward was off duty he would continue our training by taking us on long walks around the cliffs. This made us objects of suspicion to the local populace. In this sleepy Devon village everyone walked at snail's pace, going about their daily affairs, but walking briskly around for pleasure they considered very odd. Jacqueline and I sometimes thought so too but Edward made it clear that he could not abide women who lolled, so walk we did.

Apparently one of the things that made the locals suspicious was Edward's habit of stopping now and then and gazing out to sea. There never was a man who got such a kick out of a glorious view and salty air, but being observed doing this by a farmer on a tractor or a boy rounding up the cows in a field caused word to get around that there was something strange about the new people. He was blond and what about those whiskers?—the wife—now she didn't really look English; and the little girl, she was too fair—she wore her hair in little plaits tied up on top of her head—and they were always walking about the cliffs looking out to sea. Perhaps they were German spies?

At that time everyone was being urged, through posters and on the wireless, to beware of the "fifth columnists," who might be skulking about trying to pick up information that would be useful to the Nazis.

The end of this was when Edward and I decided to visit a friend who was commanding a Naval Gunnery Establishment on the coast two or three headlands away from us. It was late afternoon and we were hoping to walk there and back before dinner. As we left the village of Wembury we met an army sergeant who looked at us searchingly. Edward was not in uniform. He was wearing what we now call his spy coat, an ancient garment of greenish hue with large pockets, just right for camouflaging himself in the heather.

We walked on and on and on. I was flagging when we came round the second headland. There, completely alone, standing in front of two posts and a yard of barbed wire, was a sentry. A young soldier no more than eighteen years old on guard in the middle of nowhere. As we approached he made a rather self-conscious attempt to say "Who goes there?" or something similar, and to do the appropriate thing with his rifle. Before we reached him I said to Edward, "This can't be the Naval Camp. I can't go any further. Let's go back." But instead of abruptly turning tail I sort of waved at the young sentry and said, "This isn't the Naval Station, is it?" "No," he said. "This is the Something-something Military Establishment." "How far is it to the Naval Station?" "Three miles," I was told. Edward had been gazing out to sea while this exchange went on.

"I can't make it," I said, "we'll be late getting home." The young sentry looked so lonely. Instead of leaving at once I asked him how long he'd been in the Army and where he'd come from. In fact, we had a cozy chat, and when we said good-by a few minutes later I felt I had brought the breath of home to his tough military existence.

Edward and I retraced our steps to Wembury. Halfway there we met the same Army sergeant who again examined us with eagle eye. We said "Good evening" and walked on. As we got to the outskirts of the village we heard the roaring of an engine behind us and saw an Army halftrack gun carrier approaching us at speed. We were in a narrow lane, with high Devon hedges on both sides. Unless the driver of the carrier slowed down we'd be squashed into the bank. As he showed no sign of doing so, with one accord Edward and I clasped hands and sprinted for the nearest gateway, where we leaned on the gate and waited for the monster to pass. It didn't, though. With screaming brakes it stopped in front of us, and out jumped the Army sergeant and half a dozen British soldiers, all carrying rifles, with bayonets attached, which they pointed at us.

Edward opened the attack by saying "What the dickens is all this about?"

"Show me your papers," said the sergeant.

32

"I might if you ask me in a civil manner," said Edward.

"I have to arrest you," continued the sergeant, "for refusing to show your papers to the sentry at the Something-something Military Establishment." Our guards were closing in on us. I hated the idea of being prodded with a bayonet and so apparently did Teddy who, object though he might to the sergeant's manner, produced his papers. The sergeant apologized. The soldiers got back in the truck and we went home to dinner.

Next day we had a call from our friend, the Commanding Officer. "What have you been up to?" he said. "I have a long report here sent in by an army sergeant which begins, 'Two people, a man and a woman, were apprehended then set free last evening.'" It went on to say that the sentry, on being asked by the sergeant who we were, had said he didn't know because we had refused to show him our papers when challenged. We had asked many questions about the Naval Establishment and the man seemed particularly interested in the ships going in and out of the harbor.

The sergeant, no doubt having to explain why he had taken out a large Army vehicle and an armed guard in the middle of the evening, had written that although the man carried the papers of a British naval officer, he and the woman with him bore a marked resemblance to a couple he had had described to him in the village pub as being highly suspicious characters.

Also, he said, the fact that we ran when we saw him approach in the carrier made him feel there was more to us than met the eye and we could do with watching.

We lived down that episode and had a home in Wembury for five years, happy in all the small things in spite of bombings and separations.

When his time at H.M.S. "Impregnable" came to an end Edward was posted to various parts of Great Britain and the world, concerned with the selection and training of officers and ultimately with problems of morale, his favorite subject.

Before the end of the war he got his "brass hat"—made a full Commander.

During one of his trips to Australia, during the war, he stayed for a while at the Melbourne Club, described by him as more Atheneum than the Atheneum. When he arrived in Melbourne he had been surprised by what he regarded as an excess of hospitality, especially on the part of some of the leading restaurants in the city, when the management greeted him with deference, gave him the best table, and showered attend on him, sometimes insisting on canceling his bill. Breakfasting one morning at the Melbourne Club with another British naval officer who, though younger than Edward, was of similar height and coloring and also bearded, the other had suggested that Edward might visit him aboard his destroyer, which was lying in the harbor. Edward said he'd be delighted. "By the way, what's your name?"

"Philip."

"Philip what?"

"Philip of Greece."

Light dawned on Edward. "Then you must be the reason I have been treated so well in the restaurants round here."

"Good Lord—so it's been happening to you too?" was the rejoinder.

This was Edward's first encounter with the man who was later to become the husband of Princess Elizabeth and who is now Prince Consort. Flattered though he was to have been mistaken for the handsome Prince Philip (as who would not be), Edward was a little put out because he had been mistaken for a Lieutenant when he was at the time a Lieutenant-Commander.

Such things are important in the Navy!

At the end of the war, Edward was attached to the Admiralty in London. And for the first year of peace he continued in the Admiralty advising naval officers on resettlement, further education, and training. For the most part this meant finding jobs—the right man for the right job—for young

34

men who had given up their education or career to fight the battle against the Nazis. He had been particularly affected by their lack of prospects when he toured the Pacific and East Indies fleets toward the end of the war. He felt that these young men, far from home and worried by the thought that the men already at home might be pinching their jobs, as well as their wives, should be the concern of the administrative experts who ran the peacetime Navy.

On his return to the Admiralty from the Pacific he badgered the Admirals to set up an organization to safeguard the interests of officers of the Royal Naval Volunteer Reserve who had voluntarily (RNVR had this special connotation when Edward joined the Navy) given up to five of the most important years of their lives.

Badgering Admirals can be a dangerous sport and Edward felt he had won a great battle when one of them finally said, "All right, Whitehead, if you are so keen on looking after these chaps, set up the organization yourself." So he did.

Jacqueline and I had been forced to stay on in Wembury because the housing situation in postwar London was chaotic. Houses or flats were not to be bad. We, like everyone else, wanted to begin our lives in our own home. Jacqueline, we felt, should not be uprooted until there was some hope of getting a house or flat in London.

However, a small tragedy made us decide to leave Devonshire. A departing friend, the wife of another N.O., had persuaded me to buy four hens from her and these had become household pets. Since childhood I had been wary of hens, having once met one coming out of the hole in a henhouse when I was trying to squeeze myself through. Anyone who has studied a hen's face at almost ground level in semidarkness at a range of three inches will know what a terrifying expression they have.

But our four hens were great characters. They were housed in a small shed on a high breakwater, tucked in a corner under trees and well above the high tide mark. On seeing anyone approach carrying a dish they would run gaily along the breakwater like small boys skating with their hands in their pockets. One great *gourmande* called Effie, whose urges to lay seemed always to coincide with dinner, would lay an egg as she ran, which the next hen in line would eat before Effie realized what she had done and eat it herself.

Never did I imagine I could be fascinated by hens, but I was, and the smallest suspicion of a cackle would bring Jacq and me rushing out to the henhouse for the pleasure of picking an egg out of the nest and holding it warm in our hands.

One morning, after a night of sou'westerly gales, I poked my head out of my bedroom window to survey the landscape. There was no henhouse. I hurried into Jacq's room to tell her the news. Together we looked out of her window, which gave on to a large pond on the land side of the breakwater. There was the henhouse floating at a crazy angle right in the center of the pond where the high winds had carried it. We ran out, did some commando work dragging a dinghy over the breakwater, and rowed out hoping to find the hens hanging on to a bit of perch. But there was silence when I leaned out of the dinghy and managed to open the door. All of them were drowned. Four sad bedraggled little hens. We made the henhouse fast to the dinghy and towed it ashore in tears.

As soon as we got indoors we telephoned Teddy at the Admiralty. Between loud blubberings we told him we could not live in this place any longer. We could not imagine life without our hens clucking at us. We would rather live in one room than stay here without our foolish creatures. The decision was made. House or no house, we would return to London.

All this happened in the morning. After my telephone call I went to see the wife of the head gardener who lived in a cottage nearby and asked her if her husband would give the hens a decent burial when he came home for his dinner. Mrs. Izzard, a sweet bird-eyed roly-poly woman, promised to arrange this but later she came to see me. "Now Mrs. Whitehead," she said, "I don't want to upset you, but Jack (her husband) says it would be a crime to bury the hens what with rationing and everything. Won't you let me get them ready for your dinner this evening?"

"I couldn't, just couldn't eat them," I said, "but you can do what you wish with them," and turned my face away and wept some more.

In the afternoon our tears were dried and we were transported into a state of wild excitement when we received a telegram which announced that my young brother who had been presumed missing, but who had been a prisoner of the Japanese in Thailand for four long years, would be arriving in London the following day.

What could I produce for the reunion dinner? The hens! I dashed to the Izzards' cottage. The hens were in the larder. Mrs. Izzard plucked them and dressed them and put them in a basket wrapped in a blue and white checked cloth and Jacq and I took two of them on the five o'clock train to London.

They were stuffed and roasted and enjoyed by my celebrating family. Delicious, they said. But my tiny unswallowable mouthful tasted like sawdust.

The decision to return to London was upheld in spite of my treachery and once again we were lucky. We found a small Town house, which had been slightly blitzed, and settled down to what I hoped would be a peaceful undisturbed life.

CHAPTER 6

THIS next period, while he was busily helping fit many of these men back into civilian life, accounts for the fact that his friends and business acquaintances continued to call Edward "Commander." Being attached to the Admiralty in this postwar period, he had to leave for his office every day wearing Naval uniform—scrambled eggs on his hat and everything —a gorgeous sight, I may say.

The postman and the dustman and all the people he met as he walked down Campden Hill Road into Kensington Gardens, through Hyde Park to Hyde Park Corner, across into Green Park, over the bridge of St. James's Park to Queen Anne's Gate, said "Good morning, Commander." So it stuck.

After a year the organization was a thriving concern so Edward was able to think of leaving the Navy and getting on with his own civilian life. I must confess that when word got to the Admiral that Teddy was leaving, he said, "Thank God, we'll get some peace, he's got too much damned energy, but we'll not get another chap like him."

Having left the Navy, Edward determined to do a job that would provide satisfaction for the mind and spirit; not to allow himself to be bogged down with a job that would be only "safe." One could not live through the war without feeling that there must be more to existence than just doing a job and retiring finally to the life of a country gentleman, if one could afford it.

I was wholeheartedly in favor of this; the war had taught us how happy we could be with none of our own possessions around us, so the prospect of being partner to a man who was doing a satisfying job, rather than a well-paid one, held no terrors for me. I had always been at my best when I had had to improvise.

Edward cast about him and found a most appropriate job: running an Association, supported voluntarily by industrialists and educationalists, aimed at raising the level of education and training in industry. For a year he was happy, organizing conferences and research projects; writing and speaking to groups of industrialists whom he was trying to persuade to support this project. He was working closely with some of the most enlightened and, at the same time, successful industrialists in Britain. He put the finances of the Association in order and would possibly still be doing this job now had he not been offered a chance to serve the country's interests by heading the Industrial Section of the Economic Information Unit in H.M. Treasury. At first he refused, being happy where he was. He was persuaded to accept by Sir Stafford Cripps, then Chancellor of the Exchequer. Sir Stafford, who had heard of Edward but had not met him until he saw him about the job, was asked what he thought of the beard on his staff. His comment: "I welcome it, as long as its owner continues to be called 'Commander,' to make it quite clear that the beard comes from Plymouth and not from Chelsea."

Sir Stafford Cripps was a man whom Teddy admired enormously personally, not politically. Usually portrayed in the newspapers as an austere rather prim vegetarian, he proved to be full of the milk of human kindness. His somewhat severe mien concealed an easy controlled manner, a friendliness and accessibility rare in a man so dedicated and efficient.

Although Edward's job was nonpolitical—concerned mainly with the human factor and its impact on productivity—the disadvantages of a bureaucracy and a job in which it was almost impossible to perceive the results of his handiwork were all too apparent to him. But he remained a great admirer of Sir Stafford Cripps and it was only when the Chancellor finally succumbed to the disease he had been trying to hold at bay (by strict dieting) that Edward decided to move on.

Since Britain's greatest economic need at that time was dollars, to pay for imports of food and raw materials, he decided to find a job in a company with a dollar potential. He thought he could make a more effective contribution by earning dollars rather than by preaching from the sanctuary of the Treasury.

After considering various alternatives (a happy state to find himself in)—he joined Schweppes. The head of the company was Sir Frederic Hooper, whom he had known for some years.

It will be apparent that Edward had always been much preoccupied with his work, and we had many gay little evenings with him writing speeches, and me thinking how nice it was to have a man to talk to.

Our son Charles had been born during the Sir Stafford Cripps era, so I did have some male companionship. Actually, as I said when I began writing this, twelve years ago we were in a very pleasant groove. I sometimes wonder, had I been able to foresee what was going to happen to my life as a result of my husband joining Schweppes, whether I wouldn't have flung myself off the roof with the snow when I found myself up there alone.

One evening, when the Schweppes job was settled, Edward asked casually if I knew where his razor was. "What do you want it for?" I enquired. "I'm going to shave off my beard," said he. There was a stunned silence—until Jacqueline said, "You MUSTN'T." She couldn't remember Edward without a beard and she has told me since that the idea of his suddenly appearing with a big bald face was horrifying. She couldn't bear it; he would be like other people's fathers who were so horrid, and, most of all, he wouldn't be Teddy.

I agreed with her; men's naked faces were beginning to look ridiculous to me too. Why *do* men shave? In England many men have moustaches, and there are some beards, but when I first came to the United States, if I met an American with a moustache, he turned out to be a Canadian. Do men think they look older with beards? They don't, you know. Think what heaven it must be to have a natural yashmak to hide the marks of advancing years when they first show—round the neck.

Consider how unpleasant it is to dance with a man who hasn't had time to shave for the evening. He holds you in his arms, draws you tenderly to him, lays his face against yours. A cactus plant would be equally romantic. If in his enthusiasm he turns his head sharply from side to side with the music—some dances seem to call for this—the agony is unendurable; anyway, it is for me, prone as I am to barber's rash since the beginning of the war.

After Jacqueline's heart cry we talked about it. Apparently Sir Frederic had said something like, "As you are now joining a rather conservative firm, Whitehead, perhaps this would be the time to part with your beard." And Teddy hadn't thought of disagreeing until his two women wept all over him.

When he next saw Sir Frederic he had to say, "I'm afraid I've got a slight problem, Sir." So Sir Frederic came to see us to persuade us that we were wrong in keeping this relic of the war. Sir Frederic was a large imposing gentleman: a cross between Alfred Hitchcock and Robert Morley at his most Georgian. He had a great reputation as a debater and broadcaster on the BBC. I cannot remember what we actually said. All I do remember is that Jacq and I were determined to keep our beard and, after two Dubonnets, Sir Frederic threw up his hands and said, "You ladies have completely undermined me and I should hate to make you unhappy." So the beard stayed.

Later he said I had done Schweppes a great service by insisting on keeping the beard. But I know Teddy would have made a success of his job even without it—especially in America.

But I am anticipating. There was an interval during which Teddy had to find out how the bubbles were put in the bottles. As there was no great mystery about the process, Sir Frederic persuaded him to take over Schweppes advertising. Teddy, who had imagined his first job would be in personnel or labor relations, subjects that he knew something about, protested "But I know nothing about it." "You soon will," said Sir Frederic. During the next year or so he enjoyed himself immensely as midwife at the birth of Schweppeshire, a mythical county where everything that happened elsewhere in Britain would happen, but more so. Working with Stephen Porter, author of *Gamesmanship* and *Lifemanship* who was to do the copy, and an inimitable pair of creative artists called Lewitt and Him was exciting and amusing but at times extraordinarily frustrating. Advertisements have to be ready to meet a deadline and genius is not particularly amenable to time tables.

Schweppeshire, thus created, has continued in being ever since. Who, in England, is not familiar with Schwepping Forest, Schweppsom Downs, Schwepherd's Bush, and Schwepstow Castle? In a special advertisement entitled "Archaeolological Schweppeshire," an arrow pointing to a turret window indicated that "Queen Elizabeth schwept here"! On the ground floor was the Schwempire Cinema and two days before this advertisement was due to go to press none of those concerned could think of a movie to be named on the marquee. Edward announced this dilemma at dinner on the Friday night, adding, "By Monday morning one of us must think of the title of a film that can be Schweppified." At breakfast on Monday Jacqueline announced the result of her cogitations, "John Buchan's Thirty-nine Schweppes," for which effort she received a case of ginger beer.

A sequel to this particular advertisement, which appeared in color in the "glossies," was a letter from the owner of Chepstow Castle who said that he was delighted to see his home Schweppilloried in this manner!

After nearly two years as Advertising Manager Edward did a spell as London Sales Manager, to broaden his experience in the field of marketing; then he was made General Manager of Schweppes overseas and invited to join the Board of that company.

Well, our peaceful undisturbed existence had not lasted long, but I accepted the inevitable. I knew Edward had a bee in his bonnet about exports and now he was being given his head.

CHAPTER 7

FOR the benefit of people who still think Edward was invented by Madison Avenue, here, for the record, is the background to all this.

He was developing an overseas empire for Schweppes. Since the 1790's this venerable company hadn't trusted anyone within reach of a bottle until it was sealed and out of one of their own plants.

In India, the pukka sahib's chota-peg at sundown had, traditionally, been Schweppes Tonic. With gin, it served purposes other than the alleviation of the threat of malaria.

Nor had these attributes escaped the District Commissioner in darkest Africa. The stylized (film) Englishman, wearing his dinner jacket in the jungle, would invariably precede his evening meal with the same potion.

On the China Station the Royal Navy had long been recognized as a prime consumer of Tonic—even more of the stuff that went with it. As a Navy wife I had come to the conclusion that the faraway look in a sailor's blue eyes came not from gazing at far horizons, but from getting the proportions wrong—more gin than Tonic.

When it had become known at our sailing club that Edward was joining Schweppes, the Commodore, who had tin-mining interests on the West Coast of Africa, told us that the couple of hundred Britishers who lived and worked there remained perfectly fit so long as the supply of Schweppes Tonic held out. But if for any reason supplies ceased, they would all get sick. He was not sure that this was due to the therapeutic attributes of the Tonic, or the reverse qualities of what they drank as an alternative.

To all these outposts of the Empire, including recently

seceded oil-bearing lands where sheiks happily paid £1 ($2.80) a bottle for the stuff, it traveled laboriously and expensively from England by train, ship, sampan, raft, canoe, camel, llama, mule and, on safari, balanced on the heads of sweating bearers.

Even in the erstwhile Colonies, far away across the Atlantic, there were the discriminating few who had acquired the taste from their travels abroad, and willingly paid 60¢ a bottle for this incomparable product.

But it was apparent to Schweppes that a few Johnnies-come-lately—mostly Americans who had got into the business some one hundred years after them—were waxing fat on the proceeds of a different kind of distribution: allowing others to bottle for them in other lands; adding the water and the fizz to the far more compact flavoring shipped to them from America. So great had the international affiliations of some of these businesses become that there was talk of "Cola Colonization."

So Schweppes took its first tentative steps in this direction, in Malta. Then in Kenya, Gibraltar, and Hong Kong; all countries which the British were then entitled to call Colonies and in which the tightest possible controls could be maintained. These experiments having been proved successful, Edward was placed in charge of these world-wide operations. He went to New York to consummate arrangements by which Schweppes would be bottled in the United States of America using local water, treated to Schweppes' exacting standards; also Schweppervescence and the secret elixir, which would be imported from England.

The product was exactly the same as that previously imported in bottles and heavy wooden cases at vast cost. But some old customers refused to be convinced. The fact that the product, in bars and supermarkets, came down in price by two thirds, made them suspicious. It was essential to retain the support of this nucleus of discriminating people, with palates and pocketbooks that had encouraged them to buy the product for all these years. Even wholesalers and retailers who had imported this status symbol for fifty years said that they wanted no part of the domestically bottled product.

This move, some said, would be the death knell of Schweppes in America. Edward heard this from the lips of many of the company's oldest and most staunch supporters in principal cities in the United States which he had visited, being convinced that a personal explanation would have far more value than any kind of written communication.

Ultimately the very people who had expressed those misgivings became Edward's most loyal supporters and followed his fortunes with special interest, thus proving his faith in the value of the personal touch.

As Edward traveled the country, there were many interesting revelations. One, I recollect, was that he was constantly meeting people, as I remember in the Middle West, who had never before met an Englishman. This seemed very strange, although I suppose the reverse would have applied in a remote spot in England before the war; possibly there were people who had never met Americans, but he met people in places like *Chicago* who knew about Britain only from movies.

I, in London, received long—slightly maddening—accounts of how beautiful it all was; what a marvelous climate; how kind and generous were the American people; etc., etc. All those letters I read with a know-all expression. *I* was the one who had always wanted to go to America.

Constantly Edward flew in to London, then flew out again. Sometimes there were long absences when he went round the world and stopped off to arrange Schweppes affairs in India, Africa, Hong Kong, other places. But most of the time he went to the United States because he said he realized he could fiddle about forever in other countries and probably never see the results in his lifetime; whereas America held the real potential; it was a country that would satisfy a man's heart, and perhaps make him quite well off before he was too old to enjoy it. You will notice that, along with the desire

46

to earn dollars for Britain and his Company, he now wanted to earn some for himself as well: a thing that happens to all sensible men when, after eight years, they produce a son who will have to be educated at Lord knows what expense.

I was being kept "in the picture" (an Americanism that sounds English to me now) so that I knew what my husband was about, businesswise. David Ogilvy, whose brother Francis, then account executive for Mather and Crowther in London, had been hovering around when I first appeared before the cameras in the distant past, was head of the advertising agency retained by Schweppes in the United States. I had heard about David from Teddy and already knew his Hathaway Shirt advertisements. No one will believe this, but when I heard of some of the problems connected with putting Schweppes across with a bang in the United States—all at a distance of three thousand miles of course—my Welsh sixth sense warned me that the man who used an eye patch in an advertisement would not fail to be aware of the impact of a beard, especially when worn by a man who looked like Edward. An absolute gift! Perhaps it was telepathy and David, even as he was asking Teddy to appear in the first advertisement, was sending little thought waves of apology across the Atlantic to the innocent family of his victim and I was picking them up. Whatever it was, my Welsh sixth sense, telepathy, or sheer brilliance on my part, I was not surprised when I got a letter from Teddy asking me what I thought of the idea of his being photographed for an advertisement.

I realized what had prompted this letter. In any future discussions Edward could say that I had agreed and I should not be able to say he was vain. I could also defend this terrible action to our son when he was old enough to be told that his father had posed for a publicity picture, if we didn't succeed in covering up the whole thing before then.

Perhaps it is surprising to some people that Edward hesitated for one moment before agreeing to appear in the advertisement, but to me his reasons were clear. He felt it

47

was un-British or rather, un-English. Here he was, a man who made a success of everything he had tackled—a man who had reached the realms of top management, a man who was over forty years old, father of a family, and now it was suggested that he should become a photographer's model. It just didn't fit in with the English idea of a serious business man—it wasn't dignified! But it must be apparent by now that Edward was not a conventional Englishman. Moreover, he fully appreciated the possible value of such an unusual campaign.

The good sense of using his own image to introduce his product to the Americans was obvious since he was the person responsible, the one who would have to whip up enthusiasm among the bottlers all over the country.

So he agreed. "Just this once," he said.

The first advertisement was to be a picture of him alighting from a BOAC 'plane carrying his briefcase containing the secrets of Schweppes. The caption would explain that he, President of the American Company and a director of its English parent, had come to America to *ensure* that every drop of Schweppes Tonic Water bottled in America would be exactly the same as that previously imported from England. All quite true.

The morning the advertisement came out, Edward was living at the Yale Club as a guest. He felt rather shifty going into the breakfast room. He knew that a full-page photograph was to appear in all the New York papers, and he half expected to be drummed out of the Club in the same way that Guard officers used to have to resign their commissions if they married actresses.

He needn't have worried. Instead of being cut dead, he was greeted by strangers who congratulated him and wished him luck in his business venture. This was when Edward first became aware of the entirely different approach to selling and publicity in America.

My husband had agreed to appear in the opening advertisement only after his colleagues, Sir Frederic Hooper, Alfred

48

Steele, and David Ogilvy, had applied their best persuasive powers. He foresaw that this would mean a considerable sacrifice in terms of privacy, and perhaps make it difficult for him to fulfill his main function, running the company of which he was President. He had not committed himself beyond that first advertisement and plans had been laid for a continuing campaign that did not feature him. In the event, however, the response to the opening salvo was so overwhelmingly successful that the demand for Schweppes Tonic exceeded production. When this had caught up it was clear to all concerned that it was going to be very difficult to think up anything more effective than the personalized advertising with which they had opened, a situation which, alas and alack, continues to this day.

So Edward had to submit to being photographed in a series of luxurious settings—standing around for hours, a thing he *loathes,* and trying to conceal his lack of enthusiasm for posing and, later, acting. He had no aspirations as an actor—there was nothing of the "ham" that is supposed to be concealed beneath the surface of many men. He was not in the least abashed by having to speak to large numbers of people, or by broadcasting, of which he'd had some experience in London. But he detested, and still does, the tedium of the dumb show and the speaking of lines which were, to him, not natural and spontaneous. His attitude was one of stoic fortitude in the face of an unpalatable chore that had to be suffered in the interests of the success of the venture with which he was intimately concerned.

He did his best to observe the teachings of Confucius whom he frequently quoted in this context. "When something unwelcome becomes inevitable relax and enjoy it."

He is still trying!

In the months that followed Edward received a rash of requests for newspaper, radio, and television interviews. Some people would telephone and ask if Commander Whitehead really existed or was he the figment of an advertising agency's imagination? Edward was delighted to be interviewed to eradicate this impression and, even more important, he realized that having the name of his product mentioned in newspapers and before audiences of millions of people would go a long way toward making Schweppes the household name in America that it has long been in England.

While all this was going on I was not the wife of a sort of celebrity, of course. I was merely a wife running a home and bringing up a son with an intermittent father. I was becoming a little worried about this last aspect of it, especially when I heard the small Charles say to his father when he was at home, "Have you asked Mummy if you may do that?" Teddy looked slightly taken aback and I took cover, but this was a definite sign that I was becoming the boss of the household. And this, of course, is what people are thinking of when they say American wives are bossy. What else can they be when the day-to-day decisions of family life have to be made alone? What husband in business makes a decision without joint consultation, or at least without expert help to bring him to the point of reaching it? The fact that a businessman can now get to California in six hours doesn't mean that he spends more time with his family; he just goes to more places more often.

With all these trips away I was beginning to have to make my own life so, knowing that immediately after a short Christmas holiday at home Teddy was scheduled to go back to America, I arranged to join a party going to Switzerland to ski. Apart from America, this was my other great frustration. I had never skied. Whenever it was discussed before the war, Teddy told me I couldn't possibly go unless I could ski; there had been the war period and then I had had Charles. Since the war there had been the British Government not wanting anyone to go anywhere. It finally relented to the extent of allowing us to exchange enough money to go to Europe for a short visit, but not to the extent of giving us enough to get to America.

I was delighted to exchange letters with Teddy, telling him all about my proposed skiing trip. His first comment, as usual, was, "Darling, it won't be any fun going because you can't ski." To which I answered, "I have discussed this with other people and they have told me about the ski schools." The next letter said, "I really don't feel happy about you going off to the Alps with irresponsible people." My reply was that as Sir John Hunt, whose party I was hoping to join, had done all right on Everest, he'd probably be quite reliable on an Alp, especially as his wife and daughters were going too, as well as some other friends with considerable skiing experience.

Alas though; it was not to be. When Teddy came home for Christmas he said, "I am taking you and Charles to America with me and we are going to live there for two years." This momentous decision had been made for business and personal reasons. Teddy was becoming positively dizzy whirling round the world. No sooner had he settled a problem in Hong Kong than another would manifest itself in say, Singapore. He was laying himself down to sleep in more beds than Queen Elizabeth (the first, I mean), or George Washington in America. The beds were too short, or it was too hot, or there were mosquitoes—whatever the reason, sleeplessness was usually the reward after a long day of traveling or business talks, or both.

It was lovely for me to receive brocade from Hong Kong, brilliant red puggre cloth from Karachi, silver from Siam, bracelet charms from almost every country, even a small piece of the Taj Mahal which a workman had polished for him to bring back to me. It was lovely, but these things didn't make me happy. And neither was he happy, although he took pleasure in seeing so many countries, and he responded to the challenge of building a new world-wide business empire. On the business side the fact that North America, Canada included, held the greatest potential, and the undoubted fact that Edward's personal influence showed signs of becoming greater in America than anywhere else, supported his decision to renounce the rest of the world and to concentrate on one hemisphere.

Well, one never gets everything one wants. I pushed the Alps into the recesses of my mind and turned my thoughts toward this exciting new venture.

51

CHAPTER 8

WE came by sea. This, I think, is essential for anyone who is going to spend any time in America. One gets a proper feeling of distance and is able to appreciate the difficulties of the early settlers as the ship plunges through the gray waves of the North Atlantic.

Edward had been extremely reticent with us at home about the effect the various kinds of publicity had had on the American public so, when we had one or two recognition signals on board, and people had said, "Aren't you Commander Whitehead?" I thought nothing of it. In all modesty, we were accustomed as a family to having people look twice. Though I attributed it to the fact that we looked happy.

By the end of the voyage many people on board were aware that this was my first trip and that I was going to rise early to get the first possible glimpse of the land. When I arose at 6 A.M. and went on deck, I had a largish crowd watching my reactions. I felt rather silly because the first bit of America I saw was a gray strip of land which looked like anywhere else, and I could not enthuse. But I don't think my fellow watchers were disappointed in my reactions to the first sight of Manhattan Island. It was fantastic; a dream island suspended in space with small clouds at the tops of buildings and a pink morning light bathing the whole scene in magic. There is one passage in Dvorak's "New World Symphony" which always brings this picture to my mind.

But when we had disembarked and found ourselves waiting for a taxi, what a different world we were in. The enormous yellow painted cabs that gobbled up so much luggage; the cheerful, wisecracking porters; the chaos; the noise; this couldn't be the same magic city.

But it was. It was a different kind of magic I felt that day but it was certainly magic. We had docked early and couldn't wait to see New York. We thrilled to the sight of the man-made cliffs, the acres of glass windows, the geometrically designed avenues and streets, the size of the cars, the Hudson River—the tugboats; Central Park—the outdoor skating rinks; the policemen—goodness, they really did carry guns. The buses with only a driver to control the throng of people—the funny change thing that does a mad little dance, which Charles found overpoweringly amusing. (By the way, this is the only time I have seen a New York bus driver smile the whole time I've been in New York except for one other occasion when an argumentative woman had stumbled after she had given him a piece of her mind. I swear it, I caught his eye in the driving mirror, and he beamed.) Nothing was disappointing. The Plaza made me think of Diamond Jim. "21" and its secret vaults excited our imaginations. We could "feel" prohibition. The shops—Saks—unbelievably I was actually *in* Saks Fifth Avenue. The drugstores—still my favorite bit of Americana. (How can one resist eating at a place where one's order for a ham and cheese sandwich, with lettuce but *no* mayonnaise, on whole wheat toast, is interpreted to the kitchen as "One combo, wheat down, honeymoon." And on asking for an explanation to be told: combo—ham and cheese; wheat down—toasted whole wheat bread; honeymoon—this with some hesitation—lettuce alone without dressing.)

Above all of this a blue sky with fluffy white clouds and flags everywhere fluttering in the breeze. We did an awful lot that day—but remember, we were to be here for only two years.

After ten years of living in New York, I still feel its charm. But I must confess my first disappointment in finding that it is a much dirtier city than London. I am appalled by the amount of muck that falls out of the sky; by the way people leave garbage of all kinds in the streets—even in good residential neighborhoods—but, most of all, I am horrified by the number of dogs that are allowed to perform their natural functions on the sidewalks, while the owner stands at the other end of a leash trying to look unaware.

Of course this sometimes happens in England, too, but a friend decided to lie in wait for the culprits and teach them a lesson. The thing that made him livid was the fact that the wretched dog owners did not encourage their pets to perform outside their own houses, but waited until the coast was clear and brought them outside his. Anyway, our friend armed himself with some small logs and when the poor dog was at the moment of truth he flung one of them at him and roared in a loud voice, "Mrs. So-and-So"—(naming the dog owner whom he recognized), "*never* do that outside my house again!" Mrs. So-and-So slunk along the Chelsea street as the neighbors popped their heads out of their bedroom windows to find out what she had been doing. Presumably she did the only decent thing in future and took her dog in the park. I don't doubt the dog had problems thereafter.

I am aware of the difficulties involved in meting out this kind of justice from an apartment building in New York. Perhaps a psychiatrist (if I were in the habit of consulting one) would place an obscure interpretation on this particular obsession of mine, but, by the same token, I find it puzzling that New Yorkers, living in the most modern city in the world, should accept this hazard, smacking of the Middle Ages, underfoot.

The dirt that comes from the sky is another thing. We are now fortunate in having a penthouse in New York and I am thrilled because I can have a garden. My first lesson in economics, I think, was when I gaily ordered some flower boxes and soil—dirt to you—this being one of the words that has a different connotation in England. When the bill came it almost strained Anglo-American relations; but of course I was converting the dollars into pounds and comparing the result with what I would have had to pay in London, which was wrong of me. However, having got the boxes, I planted them with petunias and genaniums. I even went mad and had a willow tree, but I got such a guilt complex about its living a confined life in a tub that I had to kill it. Its few leaves were covered with thick, black grime and I decided I could not allow that lingering death to happen to a thing of such beauty when growing naturally.

We get tremendous pleasure out of the boxes we have left. I wake up in the morning and see the buildings opposite bathed in the same rosy light I had seen on arrival; I see the sunshine; I rush out and water the garden and roll down awnings and put out cushions and prepare to enjoy the day. We have a bowing acquaintance with the occupants of neighboring terraces and occasionally our eyes have met the eyes of other "outdoorsy" types (who live a little too far away for us to see with the naked eye) through binoculars. The green hair that the buildings sprout in the spring and summer is a source of great interest to a fellow gardener; one is curious to see what is doing so well in someone else's garden.

When we bought our apartment there were three quite large flower beds on the terrace, containing old privet trees that bravely flowered in June. The scent of privet is heavenly and, after hosing the terrace and watering the garden, it was well worth the two hours' labor involved to sit and enjoy it for five minutes.

Unfortunately the privets and the beds had to be moved. The privets had forced their roots through the roof and were making their way in a most determined fashion to the bathroom of the people living below us. Shades of Charles Addams! Experts assured us that my flower beds were too heavy for the roof and that we should have to bear the responsibility of any damage caused, so we decided that they had better go.

The resulting carnage is impossible to describe; I had no idea that so much earth could be taken out of three not very large beds. It took ages and made a ghastly mess, and one of the sad things is that, along with the earth, the mortal remains of Geordie, our pet canary (which we had buried with ceremony in an Allenbury Blackcurrent Pastille tin) also disappeared.

The terrace has a new look now; tubs on wheels so that they can be easily moved, and window boxes. It is streamlined, but this is autumn and I know that when the spring comes I shall buy perhaps just two stone urns—especially if they happen to come up for auction at Parke-Bernet—and away we will go again sinking slowly through the roof.

The snake in this paradise is, I repeat, the dirt. I have sat and watched a great apartment building belching out black smoke mixed with charred bits of paper that waft over to us and bury us like the Babes in the Wood. I have never sat for more than half an hour on our terrace without having to shower. But there are compensations. The reliable sunshine is a thing I should hate to have to do without and it is only because I had been misled by American movies and books to expect a clean city that I am somewhat disappointed. Where we live in New York, the gulls wheel in the sky and in the spring when their cries have a special note, we can close our eyes and imagine ourselves on the cliffs in Cornwall—a dream place for us.

In spite of the dirt, New York is a fabulous city. I remember flying back from Florida in February, stepping out of the 'plane and taking a deep breath. The cold air filled my lungs and made me feel giddy. I had never breathed such air. As we drove to New York over the Triborough Bridge a sign announced the temperature as 20°. This was a new experience for me too. Although England has recently suffered some snowstorms, it is very unusual. In fact, a Flexible Flyer sled which I had sent over for my granddaughter when I first got to America was used for the first time in England six years later.

The day after returning from Florida we were in Central

Park skating, walking, and just breathing. In the evening the sky turned a beautiful dark aquamarine blue; the lights shone out in the buildings; airplanes flew over flashing their red lights; and the air was cold and clear. It was electric. Who, seeing this great city, could fail to believe in flying saucers?

CHAPTER 9

I HAVE jumped my fences somewhat in writing about our apartment in New York, because it was only when the two-year period for which we had originally come to this country was up that, our stay being extended, we got ourselves a more permanent home in America.

In the meantime, when we first arrived we had to find somewhere to live. From the boat we went to an uptown hotel, the Stanhope, near Central Park and the Metropolitan Museum—an edifice I came to know very well, especially the archeological and geological sections. My son had an absolute passion for rocks—he still has—and I spent many hours peering at geods and trilobites so that when, at cocktail parties, people asked me what I thought of New York, I would mumble something about the Jurassic Age—a guaranteed conversation killer.

Gradually it dawned on me that Edward had a "public." From the very first day of our arrival in New York when the porters at the dock had crowded round calling out, "Hi, Commander" and our cab driver had turned round on his seat and said, "Aren't you that Schweppes guy?" and people in the street had muttered "Mr. Schweppes" as we passed by, I had thought that for a foreigner Edward seemed to have an awful lot of chums. Then, and I emphasize the "then," I thought it was rather sweet. Because of these cheerful greetings, New York, instead of being cold and strange and three thousand miles away from home, seemed extraordinarily friendly to me. Edward, partly because of the publicity he had received and partly because he was a lone male in New York, had been swamped with invitations and having no fond family to return to in the evenings, had accepted far too many. These had snowballed and by the time I arrived the number of invitations had reached enormous proportions. They ranged from an invitation to lunch with Sir Hugh and Lady Stephenson, the British Consul General in New York, to meet Lord Louis Mountbatten (and who could *resist?* Neither of us, since his opening remark was "Good Show, Whitehead, we're proud of you.") to a request to stop off at a bar for ten minutes so that the bartender could be photographed with Edward. As New York was the first major market in the United States in which Schweppes was launched, it was very important to make friends with the bartenders. And this part was fun too. Bartenders as a race are so easy to get on with. An invitation from Mr. Anthony Drexel Duke—gorgeous—to a day-long charity affair at Southampton for Boy's Harbor, his special charity. Dinner at the house of the fantastically glamorous 1920's flapper, his mother, Mrs. T. Markoe Robertson, whom everyone called Cordelia. English butler, silver-framed photographs of the Windsors, two ex-wives of one man meeting in a bedroom, the Mayor of New York as a dinner companion, Prince Obolensky, glistening jewels, brown legs, red dinner jackets, white teeth. Dancing in a pink-lined marquee, then the flight home in the Dukes' private plane. This was the America one had expected.

If an invitation had the remotest connection with business Edward felt we should accept, and as there were hundreds of requests for the pleasure of our company we were rapidly turning into a couple of Scott Fitzgerald characters tottering in and out of apartments on Park Avenue and houses in Sutton Place, intent on missing nothing.

We had heard of the famous American hospitality and have received a large share of it. When being entertained by friends, we can vouch for the fact that the legendary generosity to friends of friends really exists. These parties, obviously, we enjoyed, as we also enjoyed what I call the definite business parties when we would be with the people, many of

59

whom became our friends, whose fortunes were in some way linked with our own. When Americans give parties in their houses or in their gardens they are usually marvelously stage managed. My first really private party in America was at the house of Arne Fourgner, who is one of Edward's oldest friends in the United States. His habit was to give a Midsummer's Night dance at his beautiful house in Tarrytown. The spacious rooms, the floodlit gardens, the large terraces lit only by candles protected by glass hurricane shades, the special quality of the dance music, the well-groomed women, the sun-tanned faces of the men, their light dinner jackets (*such* a relief after a lifetime of being clutched to a male bosom encased in hot black barathea)—all these things seemed to me to be essentially American.—Oh—and the way the men danced. So *well!*

In England it was considered slightly cadlike for a man to dance well, but in America it is the accepted thing that boys have dancing lessons.

When Edward and I went through our dancing period we thought it frightfully *palais-de-dance* to move more than an inch at a time or to do any kind of set steps. All we did was sort of slink round the floor, but, my gosh, with rhythm. I had been tortured as much as anyone by being stuck with a dancing partner who had absolutely no idea that his feet should be doing things in time to the music—and this when the music has a good beat is frustrating in the extreme. One envies the present-day young who can gyrate through an evening several feet apart mastering the rhythm without interfering with that of their partners. Or are they missing something? Anyway, to be clasped firmly by an American male and guided through the intricacies of a samba was heaven indeed. American men are the best dancers in the world. The Arne Fourgner kind of party and similar ones in many different parts of the United States could not fail to be fun, but heaven preserve me from the kind of party to which one has been invited because one is considered some sort of curiosity. It was a little disconcerting for me to go to a "Celebrity" party and find that Edward was supposed to be one of the celebrities—and even more so for him, because the occasion instead of providing relaxation after a hard day's work became a chore from which he had to escape as soon as possible.

It took me some time to get the message about this "celebrity" business. On one occasion a lady telephoned and asked me if Edward would be at home next Tuesday. If so, would we go to a party at her house. As I was at that time bent on doing New York I accepted on the assumption that she and Edward knew each other. On consulting Edward I found he didn't recognize her name; and neither, when we arrived at her house at 6:15 on Tuesday, did he recognize her face. But he was greeted with much clutching of the arms and introduced all round. As we had to go on to another party, after a quick drink and a modicum of "polite" conversation, we thanked our hostess and left.

When being greeted by our second hostess, we met some friends who were leaving. "Good heavens," they said. "What are you doing here?" "We were invited," we said. "But," we were told, "we are just off to Mrs. So-and-So's house to meet you—you are the guests of honor."

We were covered with confusion and now realized the reason for the haunted look on our hostess' face as we left the first party, but it was now 7:30. We felt the best thing we could do was to slink silently away and hope everyone would forget. Still, we hadn't been actually *told* and we didn't think we were the kind of people complete strangers would give parties for. I should have smelled a tiny rat, because I do remember we were introduced at the first party as Commander and Mrs. Schweppes.

I did gather enough courage the next day to telephone hostess No. 1. We had a very cool little chat and never met again.

Eventually I decided that cocktail parties were not for

me. There were many reasons for this: I can drink only one gin and Tonic before dinner and stay sober; my voice was disappearing; my eyes were constantly watering; I was always starving by 7:30 and, most important, I hated to leave my son at the time of day that we, as a family, had always regarded as belonging to the children. The time between 5 and 7 P.M. was devoted to doing things like looking at rocks and stamp collections, studying foreign coins and even, when we finally acquired a television set, watching Roy Rogers and the long since departed Kukla, Fran, and Ollie, my favorites. All these things were possible for a little boy to do alone, but so much more fun with companionship. Edward evolved a frightfully clever plan whereby he could leave a party within ten minutes. I think he held the door handle all the time so he could attend when it was "business," and be home at a reasonable time. I forewent cocktail parties, but such is the life of a wife of a so-called celebrity—I don't think anyone ever noticed.

Apart from my desire to be with Charles before he went to bed, there was one other thing. I was beginning to get a tiny bit bored when, after giving my all at a party, I would sometimes come across a female who had been present, who would say to me "Oh were you there? I remember meeting your husband but—"

CHAPTER 10

WE were told that no one lived in New York during the summer and we had better get ourselves a house in the country. Another consultation and we decided that if we couldn't have a place in New York *and* in the country, we had better settle for the country. At this stage my husband's business was expanding, but I was still converting dollars into pounds and fainting daily at the result.

We heard of some real estate agents who would help us and set off on what I now call "the goon ride."

Our first surprise was to find that real estate agents, or realtors, often were women. How sensible. In England they are men, who just don't understand that you have to "feel" right about a house. The fact that they were women probably explains why they all looked stunned when we asked clever things about drains. In England, a house, especially a house in the country, is often bought and sold on its drains, many of which have been lying around waiting to give trouble for two hundred years. But in America we found the heating system took precedence and drains were rarely discussed.

We wanted a house near Long Island Sound if possible. We had studied maps and knew that there were many beaches within commuting distance of New York. As my husband was away such a lot he thought he might be able to bear occasional commuting although the thought of being incarcerated in a train for two or three hours daily filled him with gloom. Added to which he was loath to forego his daily walk to the office and become a watcher of clocks.

The agent met us at the station and as she drove us to the first house we were to look at, we told her we wanted a cottage, on the water, with a garden. The first house she showed us was closed for the winter. It had about fifteen bedrooms, a great staircase lined with animals' heads, a most depressing feeling, and a lawn of about six acres that went down to the Sound.

Number Two had fewer bedrooms, a minstrel's gallery, oak paneling (which I loathe), and an archery slit up in the flies, from which guests could be shot with a bow and arrow while sitting at the dining table. My son was just a *little* taken with that.

Number Three was filled with old English furniture; the kind one finds not in antique shops but in secondhand shops. It had an enormous meat safe (porch) filled with dead flies and piled up garden furniture. This house also had approximately twenty bedrooms, and the agent constantly referred to it as a "cottage." Since this time I have been to Newport, Rhode Island, where the really large summer cottages are, and I now recognize this understatement as a subtle form of snobbery.

After many more interesting but fruitless meetings, one agent said, "There's a really small house which will be available in two weeks' time, but I hardly think it will suit you." Why? Because, we were discovering, of our Britishness. Most of the British, we were beginning to understand, live in palatial dwellings full of antiques and pictures of their ancestors. They dress for dinner every night and sweep down noble staircases to be escorted into dining rooms where the food would be inedible. (All wrong, and especially the bit about the food.) Most of the British live in houses that have very small rooms as did the early American ones in New England. All the easier to heat, my dear!

The modern American lives in a house which is much more spacious than that of his British counterpart, and much better designed.

The American estate agents we met knew that at the other end of the scale in Britain were jolly cottagers who pulled their forelocks to the gentry and lived in picturesque thatched dwellings. But things have changed in Britain. Those same cottages are now by and large occupied by the middle and upper classes, who spend their lives trying to stop them from falling down, while the jolly cottager has gone to live in a council house subsidized by the Government.

Added to the erroneous impression that because we were British we wanted a mansion was a further false idea. Edward, as head of a company and a sort of celebrity, no doubt would want to live it up and have a place large enough for entertaining hundreds of people at once? Well, no—he didn't want that, he wanted a home for his family and, if he was to retain his sanity, a bolt hole, to which he could escape from what he described as "this celebrity nonsense," to which he had been exposed for months on end and which threatened to ruin his private life.

With some misgivings on the part of the agent, we were taken to view the small house. As we drove across a causeway to a tiny island, we saw a red wooden house with a slight Japanese look, standing on the very edge of the water, with the sea pounding against its one stone wall. My husband and I said as one, "That's the kind of house we'd like," and the agent said, "That's *it*."

We took possession of the house in Connecticut in the middle of April, and although I hate to mention it, the very first thing I became aware of when the ground unfroze and we opened our windows to let in the fresh spring air was that we had drain trouble, which was however gaily coped with by two young Italians who sang love songs quite beautifully in their native tongue while performing their unwholesome task.

We had left all our things in England and had bought simple essential furniture to use during the two-year period we expected to be in America. Everything arrived in enormous cartons in which one could have parked an M.G. These

65

were usually dumped in the garage and had to be moved before the car could be got in.

My husband, naturally, was away when this happened and I began to wonder if I lacked femininity or something. Anyway, I was always opening packing cases and being terribly tough. It was fun at that stage of one's life to be able to furnish a house completely, however simply, and, when the last carton had been opened and the contents deployed, we thought our house looked charming.

At this point I must mention one aspect of American life that still fills me with amazement, because this sort of thing still goes on.

In one of the large cartons we had received was a black wrought iron table with an oval glass top. Underneath this, at knee height, where iron strips met in the middle, there should have been a squiggle of wrought iron which would hold two flower pots. When the monster had been extricated from its container and we had read the directions for assembly and fitted all the bits together, we found the squiggly bit was missing. I telephoned Sloane's who, without any argument, said they would see to it. On the next delivery day another huge carton arrived. We were at home this time and the delivery men said, "We have orders to exchange a table." We said, "All we want is the little squiggly bit," but they said, "Ma'am, our orders are to exchange a table and we don't know of any squiggly bit." They took away our assembled table and left us with the carton. We attacked it as before and this time the squiggly bit was included. But I wondered why they couldn't have sent me the missing part, especially as we had gone to infinite trouble to assemble the table? We also wondered how many cartons we would have to unpack and explore if the second one had not been complete. The sad thing was that, when we sat round the table for the first time, with the squiggly bit in position, the two people at the narrow sides of the oval almost broke their knees on it so I had to get a screwdriver and remove it.

As time went on I would sometimes buy something which I immediately hated when I got home. But, as in England, I felt I was stuck with it; I had made a bad choice so I must put it down to experience and be more careful next time.

I mentioned this one day to a woman who said, "Why don't you return it?" "But I've had it a week," I said. "That doesn't matter," she replied. "Just take it to the service desk." I didn't have the courage to do that. Instead I packed up the garment, or whatever it was, and wrote a long, boring, explanatory letter, almost asking them to forgive me. The item was credited to me on my next month's account with no comment so, when next I made an error of judgment, I was a little braver, though not very brave. I tottered to the service desk and began my long explanations, but the garment was wrenched out of my hands; I answered a few abrupt questions and was set free.

As time goes by I find I am losing my diffidence, but I am still amazed that the stores can pay a salesman to sell an article, have it wrapped, sent out by United Parcel Service, pay someone else to answer the telephone—customer service —have United Parcel pick up the article again (sometimes calling two or three times if one is not at home) and then have someone around to put the thing back into stock. Surely this must add a large sum to the cost of the article? And I am told by saleswomen that this is a favorite sport.

Before we came here we had heard that there was no service in this country. But, after ten years, we know differently. The American housewife is treated most gently by shopkeepers. In the country one's parcels are always carried out to the car. The milkman will tiptoe into the kitchen and check that you have enough milk, eggs and cream, and will put the fresh things at the back of the fridge so that you don't use them first. Any little grocery store in New York will say, "Just call if you want anything—even if it's only a quart of milk." The American woman may have to manage a lot of the time without a husband, but the shopkeeper is always there to spoil her a little.

When I unpack anything I have bought from the mounds of paper in which it has been delivered, I am reminded of a little shopping expedition in England. To shop one always took a shopping basket. When I go back to England now, this is the first thing that strikes me as odd. Anyway, back to my shopping expedition. It was during the war, when there was a shortage of paper as well as everything else, and we saved paper bags and took them with us when we shopped. This particular day I wasn't expecting to do any household shopping; I was on my way to a party. As I waited at the bus stop I was told by another woman standing there that there was fish at Axworthy's in Plymouth. Fish was a very rare commodity and when, occasionally, a fishing boat came in with a haul the fishmonger would share it out among his customers according to the size of the family. I *had* to get some of this fish—we hadn't had any for ages. Our cottage was one and a half miles' walk from the bus stop. I couldn't go back for a basket. I got to the fishmonger and dutifully joined the queue. (This is something—a hangover from the war—that is most impressive in England; people don't barge ahead of you in shops.) When my turn came the fishmonger said, "How many in the family?" I told him and he cut off a piece of the tail end of a vicious-looking gray fish which I didn't recognize. I paid him and he handed me the piece of fish—naked. I walked through Plymouth carrying it by its tail fin, and up the gangplank of the ship where the party was being held. I changed hands when the Officer of the Day greeted me. Someone found a piece of string so that I could sling it up in a cabin away from the ship's cats and, when the party was over, I retrieved it and went home. We had it for lunch the following day. It was rather nasty.

CHAPTER 11

WE had been misinformed about the school situation in America. Every child, we were told, goes to public school, at least until he's fourteen, when some boys go to boarding school. We understood that the private school for young children did not exist, so thinking there was no alternative Charles was enrolled at the local public school.

Our son had been sent to a private school in England, one, because the English equivalent of the American public school will not take children until they are five years old, and two, because the classes were so large that we felt his education might take twice as long. Most children I have known have been dying to go to school by the time they were four years old, and Charles was no exception. We believe implicitly that young children want to learn, and love being taught, and that they can take it for long periods provided they are allowed some running and shouting occasionally, and are not trapped in a room full of used-up air.

Having previously talked to the principal of the school my son was going to attend and been assured that the children wore blue jeans (a slight change from Charles's English school where he wore tiny gray shorts with a white shirt and striped tie—the "old school tie"), we could hardly wait for the term to begin.

The school was about one mile from our house on a pleasant lane with large trees whose branches met overhead, so I decided that I would walk daily with Charles. It would be good for him before sitting in the classroom and I would enjoy the exercise. We set off, hand in hand, the first day; blue jeans, lunch-box—the complete American boy except for his hairdo which was English style, with a long fringe that fell over his forehead. We walked across the causeway, off the small island where our house stood, and set off along the tree-lined road. Almost at once there was a loud honk and a large car swooshed past us, jammed on its brakes and said, "Would you like a lift?" I said, "No thank you, we are walking." We walked a few more yards and the same thing happened. We refused a lift at least thirty times but, when we finally got to the school, I accepted a lift back home and never tried to walk again. I thought the exhaust gas of these myriad cars, containing chauffeur-mothers and sometimes quite large boys who were riding to school, would undo all the good we might get from the exercise.

On this same first day at school, Charles was asked "Are you a girl or a boy?" Speechless, he punched the enquirer on the nose and was immediately sent to the headmaster. Later, when I heard about this from his teacher, who was amused by the incident, I said casually to Charles, "I notice all the little boys have crew cuts—would you like to have your hair cut shorter?" "No thanks," he said. And that was that. He was thrilled to go along as far as the blue jeans, but no further. I have a feeling that my son was rather naughty at that school, but I put it down to the fact that he wasn't being worked hard enough. From writing a pretty good hand at five, he had to return to baby letters. From reading quite well, he had to return laboriously to the CAT SAT ON THE MAT stage. His comment on the whole thing was that it wasn't *real* school, you know, it was only *playing* school. But he cherished a soft spot for it in his heart for a long time after he had left.

The most marvelous thing happened in May. The dogwoods came into bloom. Of all the things in America, this, I think, is the most wonderful. We were taken to Greenfield Hill, where the roads are lined with these beautiful trees. The only thing comparable is a cherry orchard in Kent in the spring. I can't think why the world doesn't know about the dogwoods in America. The forsythia, the shadblow, the redbud, the flowering crab make spring in the East fantastically lovely.

If I am asked, or even if I'm not, I tell British friends to try to visit America when the dogwoods are in bloom, and to wait until they can see a country lane in July lined with exotic day-lilies. I would suggest that American flower lovers should try just once to see the primroses blooming before Easter in the woods and along the paths in Devonshire in England, and to wait until they can walk in a bluebell wood in late May. Unforgettable.

In London, on many of the street corners, there are flower sellers. One of my most pleasant recollections is of buying, on a drizzly dusky February afternoon, a huge bunch of anemones or violets. On March 1, St. David's Day, my family would buy me daffodils. St. David is the patron saint of Wales —the country where I was born—and daffodils, along with leeks, are the national emblem.

We always had fresh flowers in the house. One of the sweet sights in England is to see a workman going home on Friday (payday), with a bunch of flowers for his wife. Flowers are much more expensive in America and the central heating kills them quickly. I missed my favorite occupation of "doing the flowers"; the snowdrops placed in a low bowl on a mirror, so that one could see their reflected faces; then the anemones and violets sent to London from the Scilly Isles. The thick branches of "sticky buds"—horse chestnut—which we would cut early in the year and stand in water in a warm place so that the pale green leaves would unfurl like giant lilies; the daffodils in March mixed with pussy willow; the blackthorn sprays with their tiny starry flowers. This was reputed to be unlucky in the house, but I loved it so much that I always took a chance. The branches of cherry and apple blossoms; the wallflowers and sweet williams; the tulips, the blue delphiniums; the great bowls of roses, the sweet peas, the mixed arrangements of flowers of high summer—lupins, stocks, snapdragons; the daisies and sunflowers; the phlox; the goldenrod

71

—we had no problem with hay fever. As the year grew older, we would have asters, dahlias, chrysanthemums and Michaelmas daisies. Then the autumn leaves, whose colors we would try to preserve by putting glycerine in the water. This worked well with beech leaves. A house that had no fresh flowers looked dead to us, as though the occupants were away from home. Our final effort would be decorating the house with holly and evergreens, and, when these were removed on Twelfth Night, the cycle would begin again.

The autumn in the East in America is, I think, incomparable. In parts of England we have great stands of beeches, the leaves of which turn to heavy gold in the fall, and we would make a pilgrimage to admire them. But never have I seen color as brilliant as the maples in New England in autumn. The burning gold and red hillsides, the brilliant blue sky reflected in tremendous lakes of glass-clear water. Magic! I am not at all surprised that the original settlers decided to stay.

We still weren't used to this new life. Apart from the war period and the shortages we had endured, we also had to slough off the vague idea still persisting in our minds that it wasn't done to enjoy oneself all the time. Holidays had been short, snatched periods. For sailing in England we wore shorts and thick sweaters, enveloped by a heavy windcheater with a hood. A fair comment on the English weather is that, when my son was born on July 15, no one at our sailing club knew I had been pregnant. We *all* looked expectant, muffled as we were in oiled wool. There *were* lovely days and we *did* get brown by lying in the lee of a dune or a boat, but the weather was not reliable.

As the summer progressed in Connecticut it was sheer heaven to wear nothing but a bathing suit all day. That's the sort of place it was. We swam in water which later, to us, felt too warm.

Living as we did, on an island, we had few neighbors; they were all individualists and far too interested in their own affairs to bother about us, except in the nicest way. They told us later that they were pleasantly surprised to find that the man they had heard so much about spent his leisure in such simple pursuits. They were sure we were going to be bores because we were English. How fortunate we all were that we were not bores and they were not brash!

In spite of our happiness there, I did not escape the occasional reminder that I was the wife of a celebrity. When, soon after our arrival, I went to the local nursery to buy some plants, the young girl who served me said, "You must open a charge account." So, knowing full well that it is much cheaper to buy things on a charge account than it is to pay for them with beautiful dollars on the spot, I agreed. She looked at my signature, looked hard at me and said, "You *can't* be married to Commander Whitehead! He *must* be a bachelor—I am so disappointed." I thought for an instant of telling the girl that I was his mother, but I resisted and drove home feeling decidedly mixed up.

As the word got around we found an awful lot of cars from the mainland would have reason to stop in front of our house; the occupants would clamber on the back seat and peer over the low hedge. Sometimes I would be there sunbathing, which would be startling for all of us. We never could understand what pleasure they got out of it and feel they must have been very disappointed by the simplicity of our surroundings.

We didn't escape the cocktail party entirely either; although we found that in the country an amateur, often very good, jazz band would be added, in case the people couldn't make enough noise themselves.

I had another traumatic experience about this time. A young man came to the door and told us he was selling subscriptions to magazines. Neither Rosemary, a Scottish girl who came to the United States with us, nor I had the courage to say we didn't want any magazines, and, at that stage, we hadn't acquired the American habit of talking to people

73

through the screen door (creating the effect of a confessional); so we had opened the door and the young man stepped inside. He was a nice young man, though even to our unaccustomed ears he spoke a rather crude American. He had been to college, he said and, by selling these subscriptions, he hoped to pay for himself to go through medical school.

We wanted to know where he had been to college—we were always interested in any new American we met—and, in return, he extracted the information from us that neither Rosemary nor I had been to college. He commented that we were fortunate in being able to speak English so well without the benefit of a college education, but the big moment came when I handed him my check (I think we had subscribed to six magazines for three years—one year longer than we expected to be in America—and we got *so* tired of them). He looked at my signature and away we went again. "Is it possible that you know Commander Whitehead?" "Yes," I said, "I am Mrs. Whitehead." "Well," he replied, "how lucky you are to have married such a man without having been to college!"

I could feel the beginnings of an inferiority complex coming on. The faint stirrings of an idea that perhaps I should have stayed in England. This was the minutest flash that went through my mind, which was always dispelled when I remembered Teddy's own attitude. It was, roughly, that here was something that had been wished on him that might make all the difference in accelerating the success of his business; it was exacting at times, tedious at others, but bearable because the personal angle could soon be dropped in favor of another campaign and his own role would be quickly forgotten by the public. And the sooner the better, before someone in England connected him with the pictures in the *New Yorker*. He could imagine the comments. "What's Whitehead doing in America?—Not quite the thing, do you think, old boy?"

If Edward had looked smug or developed a little tin god complex (which is surprisingly easy when people keep telling one how—nice—handsome—clever—or even British one is) life in the bosom of the family would have been difficult to say the least. But as his one aim was to try to forget the whole thing while at home by indulging in some kind of strenuous exercise such as swimming or walking or paddling Charles's Indian canoe a few leagues (in which we all had to participate), we were usually far too exhausted to nag even if we had felt there was cause for complaint.

CHAPTER 12

AT this time we made friends with some neighbors who lived across the bay from us. Hank and Jo Strauss. They had a cruising sailboat, which Hank loved almost as much as he loved his wife. He had seen it lying at anchor somewhere in Holland and had yearned for it. And now it was lying at anchor at the end of his own garden in America.

After one or two trial day sails—*we* were on trial, we realized—we were asked if we would join them for a week's cruising to Martha's Vineyard and points North. We liked the people and admired their boat, so, in spite of the fact that I had very slight qualms about the amount of space below decks, we accepted.

The thing I would like to get across at once is that we all liked *sailing* and an engine is, to us, only useful for coming in and out of a crowded harbor. We had to join the "Doki" at New London and, as we set off that evening in a flat calm, in spite of being under engine, we were very happy.

This was a new bit of America for Teddy and me to see and we sat in the cockpit and thought about the lovely time we were going to have.

The first night we tied up at the dock at Mystic. It was dark when we arrived. When we woke up in the morning and saw the great whaling ship—the "Charles W. Morgan"—lying there, close to us, we were enchanted.

The old seafaring town of Mystic where in earlier days all kinds of ships were built, from fishing smacks to brigs, schooners, and clipper ships, is now famed as the setting for Mystic Seaport, where anyone with an interest in ships and a feeling for history—especially the history of early seagoing Americans—can immerse himself in the past.

We explored the village with its cobbled street, old buildings, and lofts; bought red-hots in the village store and admired the scrimshaw in the Museum, and if anyone doesn't know what red-hots and scrimshaw are, a visit to Mystic is indicated. We fell in love with the collection of ships' figureheads, but the thing I loved most was the schoolhouse, which had been preserved in its original state. Old desks, old lesson books, a sailor hat with streamers, the whole thing suspended in time; heaven.

At eight o'clock in the morning, we were able to go ashore, taking our washing things and towels, and have a hot shower. I don't think this would be possible in England. For one thing, you would have to anchor out in some buffeting tide and, secondly, the water would never have been hot at that time.

Having explored Mystic we set off again under power. There was some talk of hoisting the sails, in case the wind got up, but I couldn't hear very well as I was down below getting the breakfast; the sensible thing for me to be doing, as I was the one with the least knowledge of the boat, but with a wide knowledge of kitchens—

I think we got to Block Island that evening—rather late. There was certainly no time to sit in the cockpit and enjoy a gin and Tonic while admiring the sunset. We picked up a mooring (or did we drop anchor?) miles away from land, got into a minute dinghy, and rowed toward the place the noise was coming from. There were hundreds of boats, and all the occupants had gone ashore to dine on the delicious New England lobster. We had hoped to do the same but after waiting an hour in a restaurant near the quay we decided we'd better go somewhere else. Before leaving, my husband went to the Gents. He took ages, but returned just as we were about to send in a search party. He came out looking mad. Apparently, he had suffered one of two isolated instances of discourtesy in the whole of his twelve years' sojourn in America. A man who reeled in as Teddy was about to leave had seen fit to question him regarding his beard in a manner that struck Teddy as being a trifle insolent. He was told to mind his own damn business. A sharp verbal engagement ensued in which the other man—who was partly in uniform and therefore identifiable as a member of a maritime branch of the Service—found that he had engaged a vessel carrying heavier guns than his.

We walked along the dark road on Block Island looking for somewhere to eat. It was lovely really, with a fresh moist wind blowing in from the sea. It began to rain so, when a car came along, stopped, and offered us a lift, we all piled in. Teddy got in front with the two men who were already in the car and the rest of us went in the back. By the dashboard light I saw the other passenger turn and look at my husband. "Christ," he said. "Is it *you* again—er—Sir?"

We left Block Island with no regrets; though I understand it has a most interesting history. But its completely treeless landscape held little charm for us. Anyway, we wanted to sail.

We left Block Island, I repeat, and under power again. Once more we had flat calms but, this time, we had the unwelcome addition of a drizzle which, as the day wore on, became driving rain.

We decided to put in to Newport. The jazz festival was being held there. Dave Brubeck was playing. "Let's go ashore and have dinner and hear him." This was settled. After dining, we made our way in light rain to the field where the festival was taking place. We were the only suitably dressed people. Yellow oilskin trousers, slickers, and sou'westers.

We had slight livers as a result of sitting in a boat for two days, so we were all a little touchy when a group of young people began racketing around in front of us, while the star performer was playing. Words were exchanged; but the racket continued. The two brave gentlemen in yellow oilskins got up, intending to get rid of these nuisances, but Jo and I played our parts properly and led them away from the fray.

78

As we left the field we saw another group of young people standing shrouded in mackintoshes (raincoats) under a lamp. As we got near, one young girl detached herself from the group, rushed up to Teddy and flung her arms round his neck. In the jumble of hair and sou'westers and beards and rain, I couldn't see what was happening, but it had gone on for too long. I was fed up. I grasped the girl's shoulder, dragged her away with a firm "Don't be ridiculous!" and, heavens, it was the young daughter of friends. She was at summer school in Newport and was homesick for the sight of a familiar face!

Next day we chugged off to Martha's Vineyard. It was still gray and dull. Miraculously, after lunch, the sun burst out. I was at the tiller at the time so the rest of the crew, having given me directions, removed their sweaters and oilskins and went forward on deck to lie down. They slept and lapped up the sun while I drooped over the tiller, scared to let go long enough to remove my oilskins in case I lost sight of my objective.

For two and a half hours there was dead silence except for the noise of the engine. I was in a stupor.

Suddenly a breeze got up. Everybody leaped about, hoisted sails. As we approached the harbor entrance at Menemsha there were hurried discussions; the tide was running out and the harbor entrance was terribly narrow. Should we sail in? We were so frustrated by the previous lack of wind that we all agreed we must. So in we went, creeping slowly against the tide, perilously close to rocks, but sailing. Even I was exhilarated, although I had begun to feel like the forgotten woman. What a marvelous place we found. Fishing boats against the quay, swordfish tails nailed to the sides of storybook wooden cottages. A windswept landscape, bright in the sun. This was still America, but how different!

We went ashore and this time we *did* dine on the New England lobster, in a cottage overlooking the harbor. We were greeted with some awe by the inhabitants who said, Weren't we the people who had sailed in? This was sweet notoriety. We returned to the boat, feeling quite dashing. But alas, the breeze that had provided us with so much excitement in the afternoon became a howling gale. Rain lashed us. We were trapped once more below decks. We waited for the wind to abate and when it didn't, we decided to make a dash for Woods Hole. I don't remember the crossing. I was so wet. I know we sailed. But the moment we got to the mainland we hired a Hertz car and drove home in exhausted silence.

Oddly enough, the Strausses and we are still good friends.

We were given to understand that this kind of weather was most exceptional and indeed, from our own observations, sailing in the United States is not the damp and vigorous sport that it is in England. We had seen boats come into harbor in the United States after racing, with crews wearing straw hats and sunglasses, whereas a Gieves floating suit is much more in order where we had come from.

Swimming was another thing. I heard that there was a program run by the Red Cross and children could be taught to swim. I have never been a keen swimmer. Being particularly imaginative, even in a swimming pool miles inland, I couldn't be certain that something wouldn't bite me, but I had spent hours and hours standing in the water with Jacq and she was able to swim at the age of seven and a half. I must explain to the uninitiated that the temperature of the water off the coast of Devon is usually a bracing 60°. It rarely gets warmer than 65° anywhere in Britain except in the shallows during a heat wave, so it is a very dedicated Mum who will stand in the sea holding her little girl's chin up, encouraging her to kick hard with her legs, while her own nether regions are slowly turning blue. Though I say it myself.

In our first year in America I was determined to do everything American, so off we went to enroll Charles in the swimming program. It was marvelous. Quite small children were learning to swim—three and four years old—and, no doubt encouraged by his determination not to be beaten by these babies, Charles was swimming in no time at all.

While the lessons were going on I was able to study the other children on the beach. It was a mixed group—not the country club set which we later met—and as for the young people I had previously heard described as undisciplined and spoiled, I thought they were very well behaved. They were boisterous, of course, but the young always are, and on the beach and swimming, what else should they be? True, there was a lifeguard who, with one word through the loud speaker, could stop a budding water fight. The point is that the discipline was there and the children accepted it.

In all strata of society we have found American children to have extremely good manners. The only thing I hate is bubble gum, which is not only moronic but disgusting. Why is it that if you see a singularly unattractive child, with an over-fed expression and often wearing (horrors!) pedal pushers, it invariably has this nauseating pale pink protrusion sticking out of its face?

Perhaps my only real complaint about American children is that they do not give up their seats to old ladies in buses in New York. The English child may not want to but someone will jolly well see that he or she jumps to it if a lady is standing. On the other hand, I have seen American ladies accept such small courtesies with no word of thanks. When we first found ourselves in Saks, the day we arrived, I thought I had lost Charles but he had held the door open for one lady and then dozens had walked through with never a thank you or a glance in his direction and, in fact, with rather fierce expressions, so that he was afraid to let go. When I relieved him at his post, and allowed the door to swing gently shut, the final lady gave me a very nasty look.

There were many firsts for us during the time we had our rented house in Connecticut.

In England we do not use fly screens on the windows and I thought they gave American houses a blank look. In England in summer the windows are opened wide and the curtains blow in the wind—we seem to make efforts to keep flies out of larders only—that's the only place we had fly screens—and yet I don't think we had any more creatures flying around inside. Except at night, of course. One would sit up in bed reading at the Cottage with the windows wide open, and in no time there would be hosts of crane flies and May flies zooming about. I personally took notice only when a fat-bodied moth appeared, or a bat—I am terrified of bats. However, in spite of all these distractions, which we regarded as an inescapable part of country life, I cannot recollect ever having seen an English house with fly screens. They give me a great feeling of security in America although at first, forgetting the screens, I tossed many a pebble or shell out of the window, only to have it bounce back and hit me in the eye.

It was lovely to have lots of ice, but I still dislike the American habit of filling a glass with ice cubes and then somehow squeezing the drink in. That method is all right for iced tea because the hot tea melts the ice, but a gin and Tonic served that way I found impossible to cope with. All the little ice-bergs bang against one's teeth and the drink lurks somewhere at the bottom of the glass. At home we used to keep a few bottles of Tonic in the refrigerator and add it to the gin with *no* ice. I swear this is why people occasionally say that the product my husband sells in this country is different from the English variety. It isn't, you know—it's just that here it is diluted with melting ice.

We had a very small garden at our house in Connecticut but, late in the summer, I decided to indulge my favorite occupation of doing the flowers. I picked a variety of things —they had all got to the seed head stage—so, to liven up my arrangement, I entwined among the branches some long fronds of attractive creeper I had found. This work of art was placed on a table alongside a sofa in the living room and it looked lovely. Some guests arrived for the weekend. We were sitting talking peacefully when suddenly one of our guests leaped up with a startled cry, rushed to the doorway of the room, and stood there looking back at us with eyes dilated. We were most concerned. When he could speak, he said, "Poison Ivy!" We weren't sure if this was a command or a comment and, as we didn't know anyone called Ivy, we were still in the dark. Finally he told us all about it. My decorative fronds would bring him out in a rash if he so much as touched it, and this happened to most people. I was fortunate it hadn't happened to me.

Gardening gloves were brought in and long tweezers, and the offending plant was removed. We were told not to burn it because the smoke would cause as much trouble as the living plant; we couldn't bury it because it would send up little shoots and multiply. I think we drowned it. For five years, thinking I was immune, I treated poison ivy quite casually and then I unexpectedly got the rash. It was agony.

I was never long without a gentle reminder of my position in the scheme of things. There came a time when Edward and I were both invited to have dinner with the directors of an art gallery, and to attend a fancy dress ball for the students. Teddy was to be one of the judges of the costumes. This sounded fun. It was a long way from home and we had to stay overnight. I dressed formally. I was feeling just a tiny bit smug because this time I had been invited too. Dinner was most proper—white tie and polite speeches. I began to feel the complete helpmeet.

We went to the art gallery where the ball was in progress, to find that judging was to take place at once. All my dinner companions proved to be judges so they rushed away, my husband looking back at me helplessly as he was borne off by a lady judge.

I felt sort of lost. There were throngs of young people in fancy dress, massed round the center of the floor which was cleared. The tableaux which were competing would arrange themselves there in front of the judges in turn. At least, so I understood. I couldn't see because most of the people in front of me were wearing large headgear. It was the Space Man period for fancy costumes.

I wandered around the outskirts of the crowd and found a small folding chair on which I stood and tried to peer over the top. But I still couldn't see anything. Near me was a large piece of sculpture—by Henry Moore—one of his reclining things with a hole. I dragged my chair up to it and, taking off my shoes, clambered onto the raised knees of the figure. I could just see the top of Edward's head. As I sat there a young man came along (he was a photographer who had taken some pictures of us when we arrived): "Aren't you Mrs. Whitehead?" he asked in shocked tones. "Good heavens, no!" I said. "What would she be doing up here?"

CHAPTER 13

SOON after Labor Day, the first year we were in America, we were dining with friends in New York. Among the guests was a large man, six foot six and broad-shouldered to boot with sleepy eyes and a most beguiling manner. His name was Jim. Jim lived in California and when he heard that, because of problems with the Bank of England, I might have to leave the country without seeing his state he was horrified. He said, "I am picking up a new car in Chicago the day after tomorrow and driving to San Francisco; you must all come with me. Teddy can relieve me driving and he can do some of his Schweppes business on the way." I said, "Of course—wonderful—how marvelous!" And dismissed it as party conversation. However, the next day I was telephoned by this gravelly voice which said, "I've made all the bookings on the flight to Chicago and we leave tomorrow." I began to make noises about Charles who could not be left behind; the journey would be too much for a little boy, etc., etc. Jim said, "Don't let it bother you; the whole trip will be arranged round Charles and we will stop whenever you think we should."

No mother of a family preparing to cross the country in a covered wagon could have felt more adventurous than I as I got into the back seat of a new Ford station wagon in Chicago. With Jim at the wheel we left early in the morning and pointed toward California. After a short time I began to realize that I had lived a very sheltered life on the little island in Connecticut. California was a long way off but I felt we were going to get there in a very short time. We went like mad. When Teddy and I told Jim that in England all new cars are "run in" very carefully for the first five hundred miles, not doing more than 35 m.p.h. and then gradually increasing the speed for another five hundred, he said, "Oh, we don't bother with that; the engines are 'run in' in the factory and the great thing is to get them loosened up." And off we would go at the speed of sound. Jim would turn to me in the back and say, "Now, do let me know if you and Charles are hot or cold or in any way uncomfortable." I would be so anxious to have him look back at the road, and also I didn't like to tell him at that stage that I was frightened, that I'd say, "Everything's wonderful." However, when in Springfield, Illinois, the engine suddenly boiled and we had to stop, my feeling of relief at the respite was tremendous.

I have no doubt we would have gone through that town like a flash, had it not been for this happy chance. As it happened, I was able to see, for the first time, a classic American Middle Western town.

We had come to rest outside a large white house—wooden, of course; we still weren't used to the idea of wooden houses, and this was the largest I had seen. Jim said casually, "That's the Governor's mansion." "Goodness," we said, "do you mean Adlai Stevenson lives here?" Jim was surprised by my excitement, but for me it had all the thrill of seeing history at first hand. I had read a lot about American politics and I had seen Adlai Stevenson on television and admired him greatly, so, if the White House is, say, the equivalent of Buckingham Palace, this was like seeing No. 10 Downing Street. As we stood there, absorbing atmosphere, Mr. Stevenson himself was driven out of the gates; my trip was already made.

We saw our first Capitol building and discovered Lincoln's tomb—Lincoln! A man as well known to English children as Winston Churchill is to American children today.

We wandered around, admiring the houses and the broad tree-lined streets. I love this aspect of old American towns.

We didn't have much time; Jim was anxious to get under way and our impressions are necessarily fleeting, but we were so glad that the Ford had provided us with the time to see this interesting old town. We drove off and got to St. Louis literally as the evening sun went down.

More capable observers and recorders than I have written travel books about America, so I won't attempt to do anything but record a few things that struck us as odd or interesting or amusing.

We were traveling very simply and staying at motels, there being no alternative, I believe. Apparently there are motels and motels, but Jim knew the best ones, right across the country, so our impression was that they were extremely efficient, clean, and hygienic. We would get up early in the morning and drive for two hours before breakfast, thereby getting a lot of miles done before the traffic got heavy and before the sun got too hot. Teddy, accustomed as he is to a lot of exercise, was finding it hard sitting for such long periods, and spent an awful lot of time trying to find somewhere to swim. Jim would, not very willingly, stop when we saw a sign saying "Swimming Pool," but never, not once, although the temperature was at times over 110°, did we find one with water in it. Why? Because it was after Labor Day. Quite mad!

We realized we were in the "Bible Belt" when, in Tulsa, Oklahoma, a man whom Teddy had asked for directions to the nearest swimming pool tried to convert him to some obscure sect of Christianity on the spot.

We speeded for days along roads as straight as the old Roman roads in England, but infinitely longer. The corn had been cut, so all we saw was a great expanse of stubble for hour after hour. This I think was Oklahoma. We knew we were in Kansas when we saw baby "twisters" in the distance. (By the way, when later I mentioned "baby twisters" to my daughter, she thought I was referring to a peculiar Middle Western religious sect that twisted babies.) We saw tumbleweed blowing across the road and, in the various homemade notices on garages and little wayside stores, we saw many signs of illiteracy, which made us realize that America is not entirely English-speaking; to many of its people ours is a new language.

We were crossing the Panhandle of Texas and now we came to grazing country with, we thought, rather sad little steers dotted around. We were still remembering the fat animals nourished by the lush green grass of England.

Teddy was driving on the Sunday morning. Egged on by Jim, he too was trying to loosen up the car. By this time he realized he wasn't going to get a swim until he got to California, so he wanted to waste as little time as possible in the wide-open spaces. Jim had discouraged walking across the plains. Rattlers, he said. So, apart from tottering into a motel and some necessary shopping expeditions in one or two towns, Teddy had no exercise.

It was a very hot Sunday morning and we were miles from everywhere, when, suddenly, the car stopped. No petrol—gas. The gauge, which Teddy swore had registered a quarter full when he had taken over the driving, had suddenly flipped to empty. Jim looked at Teddy with his sleepy eyes, and Teddy knew it was up to him to get us moving again.

Charles and I got out of the car and walked up and down the grass verge. Charles shot his little Indian bow and arrow, happy to be free. Jim reclined in the car. Even he had to accept the fact that we couldn't get to California without petrol.

I saw the gleam in Teddy's eye. The last gas station we passed was twenty miles away. As an old walker he was game to try—gosh, it would be a relief to walk. Jim, however, made dark remarks about walking in the heat, and it *was* hot, so Teddy decided to wait for a lift. Several cars passed but all of them ignored Teddy's waving arms, though some of them waved back. We knew hitch-hiking had been invented in America, but Teddy just did not have the technique. He held his petrol can in his hand and waited. Finally a car did stop and Teddy got in and was borne away. He told us afterward that, when he saw the occupants of the car, he almost refused the lift. There were at least seven of them. Swarthyvisaged, and obviously continuing a party that had begun the previous evening. As Teddy squeezed himself into the car nursing his petrol can there was silence for a short time. No doubt the occupants were wondering what strange apparition had appeared on the plains of Texas. But Teddy's efforts at small talk, though probably not understood, at least had the effect of assuring them that he was human. So, as the car started off again the singing was resumed, accompanied by much passing of the bottle. On the insistence of the driver who seemed likely to take offense, as well as his attention from the road, Teddy took a swig, and by the time the petrol station was reached, they parted the best of pals.

The petrol station comprised two pumps, a shack, and a "yep" type of character, who was filling the tank of a car in which sat a young man and woman. To Teddy's "Will you fill this petrol can for me please?" the man answered "Yep," and to his "Is it possible to get a taxi to take me back where I came from?" the man said "Nope." A remarkably difficult man to converse with, Teddy thought. At this point the young man in the car leaned out, and said "Are you English?" "I am," said Teddy. "Get in, I'll take you where you want to go." Teddy demurred because the car was pointing in the wrong direction. However, the young man insisted. "As you're English," he said, "I am delighted to be able to repay in a small way the many kindnesses I received in England when I was there during the war." He was a young school-teacher. When he got Teddy back to his marooned party, the young man assured us all that he was delighted to drive forty miles out of his way to help an Englishman. He had been on his way to Sunday lunch with his mother-in-law, but we were to think nothing of it. We wrote down his name and address meaning to write later and thank him again, but as fate would have it we lost the bit of paper and all the young man had from us was silence. If there is a mother-in-law somewhere in Texas who is still mad because her son-in-law was late for Sunday lunch about ten years ago, we would like to let her know that we were responsible and we're sorry.

Charles had been longing to see a real cowboy and, on the same Sunday morning, we stopped at the next town to fill up with petrol. Town, I said. Actually it was a wide-ish road, lined with rickety buildings; a real one-horse affair. There was a gas station, and opposite a neon-signed "eatery." In this eatery was the tallest, slimmest, handsomest, blue-jeaned, cowboy-booted and cowboy-hatted character we had ever seen. The fact that he was toying with a thing like a chocolate milk shake did nothing to destroy the picture. Charles gazed at him in awe. I wonder if the man knew what a sensation he was causing. We had difficulty in leaving that place. On getting up I found my foot had been resting on the largest piece of gum imaginable. I couldn't move until someone came along with a knife and sliced me away from the floor.

We saw the Painted Desert in Arizona. Early one morning, with a sharp wind blowing, we admired the purples and pinks and blues: utter magic. We tried to ignore the empty beer cans around our feet. Why do people throw beer cans on the ground when there is a garbage container within two yards of them? Beer cans take twenty years to disintegrate, I am told. People distribute litter at beauty spots in England too, of course, but it's usually toffee papers, not beer cans, and they are not as offensive. This sin is perpetrated by people who don't give a hoot about anything anyway. But here in America we have continued to witness otherwise civilized people throwing papers and cigarette packets out of car windows, if not beer cans.

The sad thing is that this is the sort of thing one is apt to remember, even at a place of such indescribable beauty as the Painted Desert.

We made a detour and went to the Grand Canyon. Looking back, we don't know how Jim allowed us to do this. We can only think that we had covered so much ground at such speed that we had a day in hand and he may have found he was approaching California ahead of himself. No, I am being ungenerous. Jim, knowing of Charles's passion for geology, was determined that he should see this geologist's heaven.

We didn't have time to do the mule trip into the bottom of the Canyon, for which I am eternally grateful, having since been frightened to death by a Western pony called Breezy which insisted on looking over the edge of a cliff with me on its back. We gazed and gazed in wonder at this phenomenon. One could somehow see how the world began.

We saw our first Indian village and real Indians. Charles began to wish he'd had a hair cut after all, when a warrior with a tomahawk in his belt seemed to be eyeing him with interest. The young braves did a rain dance exactly the way we had done it as children when we played cowboys and Indians, nearly six thousand miles away.

They then did the eagle dance and, as the male dancers raised their arms, I noticed that the feathers covering their manly chests were sewn onto pink brassières. How sweet!

We had a taste of driving across the desert along roads that vanished into the sky miles and miles away. There were extinct volcanoes, lava fields, and the skeletons of cars that had given up the ghost and had been abandoned by their owners. What had happened to the occupants? We met no other traffic and we prayed that our chariot would develop no problems. We had the windows fixed so that we had the maximum amount of air circulation in the car. I had noticed people driving with one arm outside the car and holding onto the roof. This had puzzled me. I thought it looked moronic, that the drivers were showing off, rather like riding a bicycle with no hands. But crossing our bit of desert, I soon realized why they were doing it. We all had an arm outside, and the rush of air blew up our sleeves and down our sides—perfect air conditioning.

Occasionally Jim allowed us to rest at an oasis in the real heat of the day and resume driving in the cool of the evening. Charles has never forgiven us because he was allowed to remain fast asleep when we passed through the land of the giant cacti. In the dusk we rushed past their rather frightening shapes. Huge things, forty feet high. Jim told us how the desert blossomed in the spring—we must go back to see it.

CHAPTER 14

SUDDENLY we were in California. It still looked the same —arid desert—but Jim perked up. This was home, but he wasn't going to get really enthusiastic until we got to San Francisco where he lived. As it was, we were heading for the Beverly Hills Hotel. We had been fascinated, educated, over-whelmed, and exhausted by the nature in the raw we had observed; now we wanted all the luxury we could afford. We were approaching the home of glamor; the place where the movies were made, from which the rest of the world had formed their (quite wrong, I now realized) impressions of America. But the glamor was still there, and I was prepared to lap it up.

To go back to this question of impressions made by movies. Although I was old enough to know better, I had allowed myself to be influenced by the film image. Most of the Amer-icans we had met during the war were naval personnel, and there is nothing more becoming than a naval uniform. Among our particular friends were the officers of a control ship which was in Plymouth before the invasion of France.

On Sundays a few of them, often including the Admiral, would be driven to our cottage in a jeep. The driver was a tall, slim boy called Joe who wore his jumper and trousers like a second skin. When he wore his pea jacket, with his hands tucked into the high side pockets and his white dough-boy hat tipped over his forehead, he was the perfect picture of an American sailor. The other members of the party would arrive in terribly smart work clothes and of course the naval cap, which is so becoming to a man.

Their reasons for coming were to get away from the ship for a while, and to help us saw wood for the fires (coal being rationed). After sawing like mad, we would have tea and, good heavens!—brown bread and peanut butter and treacle. (I think the peanut butter was part of American lend lease.) We would listen to some music on the gramophone and then our guests would pile into the jeep and go back to their ship. Strangely enough, although I can well remember everyone, including the Admiral, sawing wood and boasting about the amount he had cut, I don't remember Joe, the jeep driver, ever taking that kind of exercise. He had an absolute passion for a small Chinese sampan we had moored at the end of our garden. This little sampan, painted in traditional Chinese colors and with a devil's face on the prow, to frighten away evil spirits, had been brought from Hong Kong by a British naval officer and we had bought it from him. It was propelled by a long sweep over the stern. There was a certain knack to working this, but once one had mastered it, the little sampan rocked through the water at great speed.

Joe spent all his time, first trying to work it, and then darting up and down, calling to my little daughter to take pictures of him. Because of his addiction to the sampan, he was probably the only one of that group who had any real contact with the sea during the whole of the war, modern ships being what they are.

One particularly charming member of this group of officers thought of my little daughter during what must have been a very hectic time off the coast of France on D-Day—plus either one, two, or three—I am not sure which.

He told me that while his ship was standing by, having put supplies ashore, he saw a lovely little varnished dinghy lying in the water, obviously abandoned. He remembered that Jacq wanted more than anything else a dinghy of her own, so, without more ado he got a party of sailors to haul it on deck.

Thereafter, they had a rather busy time, what with enemy planes and so on, but occasionally he would check that Jacq's dinghy was still aboard.

Alas, when they got to Plymouth the dinghy had disappeared. On investigation, he found that another officer, not knowing the story of the dinghy and noticing that its planking was opening up in the sun, ordered it thrown over the side. Within sight of Plymouth. How maddening—it would have been such a thrill for Jacq to learn to row in a little dinghy that had been in battle.

Conditioned by these nice young men and the films, I thought all Americans would be handsome and charming.

I hadn't been prepared for the "un-American" look of people in New York. So many of them looked foreign, and, in the streets, rather bad-tempered. We had seen our one, we considered, typical cowboy when driving across America, but here we were in California and up to now no one had looked particularly glamorous (except for Jim, of course). But the Beverly Hills Hotel, that was another matter. Almost everyone was handsome or beautiful—their handsomeness or beauty enhanced by the occasional squat swarthy gentleman, who just had to be a movie mogul.

One tiny fly in the ointment: it was here that I saw for the first time a girl in public with her hair in pincurls and a hair net. She was a lovely girl with a fabulous figure and she reclined alongside the pool. I thought that whatever she had had covering her head had blown off unawares, and I wanted to let her know about it discreetly in the way that one would tell a woman if her slip was showing. But Teddy said, "This, oddly enough, seems to be the habit—I find it most off-putting." Perhaps I should be grateful? One fails to understand the misguidedness of females who appear before their husbands in curlers or who will go to bed with metal fortifications on their heads. When I was a young woman living in my boarding house in London, I was once surprised by a young man who entered the bathroom just as I was stepping into the bath. I had been washing and setting my hair, and had parceled it in one of those horrid hair nets with elastic all round which pressed one's eyebrows down.

94

Before the young man withdrew, which was almost at once, instinct made me whip off my hair net, and only then did I leap for my bath towel with small shrieks. The incident proves something—I know it taught me to check the lock on the bathroom door!

But back to the American male.

A young man called Coleman Morton, who lived in California and whom Teddy had met at the Yale Club, had asked us to go to his house to meet his family. He was going to pick us up at our hotel and drive us to Pasadena where he lived. We walked to the entrance, and there was the, to me, perfect American. Tall, athletic looking, brown face, white teeth, fair hair cut short in that style which is a cross between a crew cut and Julius Caesar. He was waiting for us. He drove us away. I wanted to preserve him as the perfect specimen. He had a most attractive, sweet wife, four beautiful brown children, a charming modern house, a kidney-shaped swimming pool. How American can you get? After a little while some other guests arrived. One was our friend's brother. He was tall, athletic looking, brown face, hair cut short in that style which is a cross between a crew cut and Julius Caesar— but he was dark. His wife was most attractive and nice. I heard he had four or was it five delightful children, etc., etc.

So these people did exist. I got as much of a thrill out of seeing them as I had out of the Grand Canyon.

One thing I had to do when I got to Los Angeles was to contact an aunt who had lived there for fifty years. She was my mother's sister, and she had come to the United States as the bride of an American. My mother has since told me that when her sister announced that she was going to marry an American all the younger brothers and sisters, of whom my mother was one, burst into tears, imagining that she would spend her life in a covered wagon resisting Indians.

My aunt sailed away and for the next fifty years letters were exchanged but she did not see any of her family. When she left she spoke very little English. My forebears are Welsh, and at that time—now sixty years ago—Welsh was the language spoken in Wales, especially in the more remote parts of the country.

We had only one whole day in Los Angeles so I had to move fast. I found the telephone number in the book, only to learn that the 'phone was out of order.

My husband had already left the hotel to go about his business, so I had to make my own decisions. I decided that having come six thousand miles I could not allow myself to be beaten at this stage so I consulted the doorman who told me that my destination was a long way away. A taxi would cost the earth. I must get a bus outside the Beverly Hills Hotel—change at Hollywood and Vine—I remember that very well—I forget the rest, but I was to take another bus, then take a taxi for the final stage of my journey.

Charles and I enjoyed jogging along in the bus after our wild, wild dash across country. All those expensive-looking houses so close together!

Then at Hollywood and Vine strange beings in pedal-pushers and sun glasses, and although it was morning, very revealing blouses with extremely uplifting brassières. As Charles was only five we wasted very little time there and soon found ourselves at the end of the second stage of our journey.

Now we had to find a taxi. We were in a pleasant suburb. There were cars parked in driveways, but not a taxi in sight. In New York the yellow painted taxicabs were so numerous.

We walked along hoping we were going in the right direction, and finally I spotted one. It was painted yellow and it stood outside a garage and there was a man looking into the engine. I walked up to him and said, "Will you take me to this address, please?" He looked at my little book and said "Why sure." He shut down the bonnet, and opened the front door of the car for Charles and me to get in. This was unusual, but I thought it must be part of the relaxed California living I'd heard so much about. As we drove along, we told him about our trip. On arrival at our destination, I began fumbling in my handbag and as there was no meter I said, "How much do I owe you, please?" He said "I am not a taxi—I was filling up with gas at the garage. I knew you were from England the moment you opened your mouth. I spent part of the war there, and I am only too glad to do something to repay the many kindnesses I received in your country." I was embarrassed but it was so heart-warming, especially as this same little speech was being made to us for the second time.

When Charles and I walked up the path toward the front door a woman came out of the house and stood on the porch. My aunt, my mother's double, and when she spoke her voice too was the same as my mother's. A soft Welsh voice speaking English with a Welsh accent. After sixty years.

"You must be Sarah's daughter," she said. "You look the way I thought your mother would look when she grew up."

We sat in the garden under a palm and ate an orange, tree ripened, warm in the sun, and reminisced. After so many years away from any of her blood relations, what did my aunt want to talk about? Not family history, nor the changes in Wales, all these things she knew about from letters and newspapers. What she really wanted to know was if my mother had told me of the good times they'd had as children. Did I know about the house on the banks of the River Tiefu? Had I heard the story of the dog saving its puppies when the river flooded by putting them in a bowl and swimming behind them until they were rescued? Did I know about the time they had lifted a man's toupé off in chapel by lowering a gooey piece of homemade toffee tied to a string from the gallery where they were supposed to be singing in the choir? And the punishment they suffered as a result? Had I heard about the horse eating a large piece out of an older sister's tulle and roses hat while she sat elegantly, she hoped, in an open carriage flirting with a swain?

I had heard them all and could even remind her of some things she had almost forgotten.

"Oh, it's been lovely talking about these things," said my aunt. "You must come and see me again." But that was the last time, because very soon afterwards she died.

Our next port of call was San Francisco. We went to Jim's home, met his family. Divine, naturally, then Virginia, his wife, took me to a woman's luncheon. I don't know if this phenomenon exists in England. I don't think it does. One would sometimes meet a woman for lunch at a place like Fortrum's but these were always rather hurried. Somehow one didn't sit around for hours in entirely female company. The only all-female activity I can remember is the Mothers Union, and these were mostly village affairs lasting about one hour, most of that hour being taken up with the making and drinking of tea and having a lovely gossip about what happened to Mrs. So-and-So's daughter who went off to be a typist. They did exchange knitting patterns and recipes, but the real object of the exercise was the chat. Perhaps the luncheon in San Francisco was not so very different because there *was* a lot of chat but I didn't join in because I was so interested in looking at the women around me. We had to be at our tables by twelve—a fashion show was to be held and as the beautiful Virginia was modeling, we had to get there early, so I had lots of time to watch.

Everyone ordered drinks. Drinking was to me (and still is) something you do with a man, but as everyone was having Martinis and things I valiantly ordered my gin and Tonic. That was my second mistake. My first had been to wear an English suit, which nearly killed me. The temperature in the large room must have been 100°. But apart from my physical discomfort, I was enjoying myself. I hadn't seen so many women so dressed up in years. They all wore hats and gloves and earrings and bracelets and veils, and rings, and furs over the backs of their chairs, and they were much more formally dressed than any other people I had seen in America. I have been back to San Francisco many times, and I think it is the only city in which I feel I *should* be wearing a hat.

We had so little time and we were determined to see as much as we possibly could so when my husband disappeared in the morning Charles and I set off to explore the city.

We had been told about the glorious view from "the top of the Mark"—but at that stage I didn't know what "the Mark" was. I imagined it was some sort of landmark. We took a cable car to the top of the hill, but we found the view was obscured by the tall buildings so I stopped a young woman in the street and said, "Excuse me, could you tell me where to go to see the view." She looked puzzled for a moment and then said, "I'm sorry, but I don't speak French."

Bemused, I accosted another woman, who also apparently wondered what language I was speaking, and as we stood there flapping at each other, a gentleman joined us and said, "May I help you?" "Please don't bother," I said. "I only want to find the place up here where one can see the view." "Come with me," he said. Charles and I followed him docilely, but when he walked into a large apartment building I said, "Where are we going?" "To see the view," he said. "I have an apartment on the eighteenth floor here which has the best view in San Francisco." I had to make a quick decision. Ten A.M. seemed a pretty innocuous time. Charles was with me, people didn't usually "pick up" females with attached small boys who might turn out to be menaces; the man looked terribly healthy and happy, and anyway I had been grown up a long time. In the apartment his wife was putting some clothes into a suitcase. She looked surprised when we arrived. We were ushered into a sitting room which had a wide window overlooking the most glorious view.

Charles and I stood and admired it as long as we decently could, then we said "Thank you very much," and left. I don't think we introduced ourselves. I wish we had.

We took the boat ride around Alcatraz Island and under the Golden Gate Bridge. There were lots of passengers, obviously visitors to San Francisco or they wouldn't be doing this. A woman sitting next to me said, "Are you English?" and when I admitted that we were she turned to the rest of the group and said, "What do you think—they're English," and for the rest of the trip we had to answer questions about the Royal Family, and so on, not that we knew very much, but, they said, they just loved to hear us talk. I don't think our guide cared for the competition.

We were going to fly back to New York but first we had to go to Phoenix, Arizona, where my husband had some business to attend to.

Phoenix is as improbable a place as it is possible to imagine. What picture would be conjured up by this place name in the mind of an Englishman living in, say, Harrogate, Yorkshire—or Cheltenham, Gloucester? Could he imagine flying in across endless deserts; no visible rivers, no sea within several hundred miles, no mineral wealth, no natural resources, or other apparent reason for being.

To reach it (by air is I understand the only sensible way) one has to fly over hundreds of miles of inhospitable-looking country, a vast burning desert with occasional outcrops of bare dark brown sandstone, looking like pebbles from forty thousand feet, but more like mountains from ground level. But when one arrives at the fine modern airport this thriving city turns out to be as hospitable as any in America. The people? What are they doing there? Hardly any of them were born there, but, during the last decade, particularly, they have been flocking in from all over the United States. Why have they come? To escape from the cold, the ice and snow, and to revel in the hot, dry sunshine.

Insofar as a parallel is possible to conceive, the inhabitants of Harrogate and Cheltenham would be the British equivalent. Many of them retired. Most of them seeking a healthy climate—though, of course, a completely different kind of healthy climate. In England, hot and dry is a climate that is unknown. Harrogate is definitely bracing, swept by gales from the North Sea, whereas Cheltenham has a softer climate. Wetter.

We heard all about Phoenix from a young business associate of my husband. I remember a broad avenue of royal palms, and we were told that anyone struck by a coconut falling off a palm tree would be suitably rewarded. We saw dates growing, bought some and ate them. How different from the variety we used to have at Christmas time at home, squashed into a little coffin by, I always thought, Arabs using their bare feet.

We were shown a house sitting out in the desert. A round house with a broad ramp spiraling round the outside. Taliesin, the house designed by Frank Lloyd Wright for his son. A star pupil showed us this creation of his master, and also some houses that he himself had designed. They were completely modern, and yet to us they looked medieval. Perhaps it was moon architecture; it was certainly imaginative and mysterious.

The English are passionate gardeners, and in Phoenix of all places we found our counterpart. Everyone, we found, cherished a garden. At the very least, a patch of green, very green grass shaded by a few date palms. But at what cost, in terms of time and trouble, as well as money, was this achieved! The lives of the residents were regulated by their gardens.

Going to dinner one night, at a most improbable restaurant called The Robin Hood, we were met at the gates by a "knight" in chain mail on a white charger. He took our names and galloped ahead of us to blazon forth the news that there were strangers at the gates and to bring on the boar's head. We ordered steak—we were *always* being told we were now in the restaurant where the best steaks in the United States were served. During dinner, we noticed our host glancing surreptitiously at his watch. We hadn't thought we were all that boring. After a while, we had to say, "Shall we leave?" He said, "I'm awfully sorry, will you excuse me for fifteen minutes—I have to go and turn on the irrigation. If I miss it my garden will dry out before my turn comes round again."

A system was fixed by the water company, and people took it in turn, sometimes having to get up in the middle of the night to preserve their precious plots. And we British think we take pains to cultivate our gardens.

CHAPTER 15

WHEN summer was over and we could no longer sail and swim, Edward's thoughts began to turn toward hunting—with hounds, not with guns. We didn't play golf, feeling this was a game for rather elderly people, and, at that stage, we were in America only on a prolonged visit so we belonged to no country club. Edward had regularly ridden over the Pocantico Hills with friends when he had been in America alone, and when we established ourselves in our house in Connecticut he was able to do some fox hunting with the Fairfield County Hounds, a thing we never thought we'd find within sixty miles of New York.

Unwittingly I had been the means of introducing him to what I am told is about the best fox hunting in America.

As we were making my first crossing of the Atlantic we ran into bad weather which meant that the Whiteheads were not always on deck at the same time.

While I was taking the air alone one day I fell into conversation with a fellow passenger. I had noticed him previously with his family, and the thing I had particularly noted about him was that he was wearing a beautiful Irish tweed jacket with the collar turned up in what I considered to be a horsy fashion. Well, on this occasion his family was below decks and so was mine. We paced the deck together and he told me he had been to the Dublin Horse Show.

Instead of changing the subject at once, I launched into a horsy conversation. Since my Pippin day the only horse I had been in contact with was a gentle pony called Gypsy, which Jacqueline had had for a while during the war, and I should explain that horses to me are still lovely only to look at but terrifying to know, and no amount of persuasion on Teddy's part could get me nearer to a horse than the other side of a large fence.

However, I had been close enough to the fence often enough to be able to keep my end up in a conversation of this sort so I allowed this nice American to think I was just mad about the dear creatures.

The next time we met, we went on to hounds, I think—anyway the whole tone of our conversation was terribly Jorrocks and having got involved I couldn't retract.

All the members of both families met eventually and, with Teddy there to keep up the horse conversation, it wasn't such a strain for me.

We all got on with each other terribly well, and when we were saying good-by they said, "We have a farm in Pennsylvania in the Unionville country—you must come and have a day with us!" I felt quite safe, not at that stage having learned that Americans mean it when they say this sort of thing. I thought I'd never be found out. However, soon we *were* invited for a weekend. On the 'phone we were told, "Bring your hunting kit—we can mount you." I hurriedly said I wouldn't ride, and secretly hoped I'd get through the weekend without being discovered.

Having been driven twenty miles or so from Wilmington, we arrived at Windfall Farm, the beautiful Georgian home of Clem and Marcia Hoopes. A house full of dogs and flowers, which had all the character and charm of the nicest kind of English country house, but with the added joy of central heating everywhere.

The barns surrounding the farmyard, one of which had an ancient hex sign on its gable, were essentially American, quite different from English barns, but the fat pigs in their pens grunted just like English pigs, and the cows in their stalls mooed with no trace of an American accent.

At the meet next morning Edward was well pleased to find that this was indeed wonderful hunting country, mostly grass, with every fence clearly jumpable: no wire to be seen.

Whilst everything was according to Hoyle—every bit as formal as in England—the people we met, including the lady Master, were welcoming and friendly. A great day, said Edward.

And another pleasant thing about it, nary a reference to Schweppes—Oh! the bliss!

My guilty secret was discovered, of course. Marcia and I followed the hunt in a jeep, which she drove relentlessly across country, through streams and gaps in hedges, down steep slopes and across beautiful wide fields. All the time I was being entertained by a commentary on the hunting. When I was told we should, with luck, join the field at a point where they would probably check, I hoped the jeep would refuse a fence or something!

We were there when they checked. I stayed inside the jeep as long as I could, but finally had to get out. Marcia and I draped ourselves against the mud guards. My one thought was to have only one side of me exposed in case a horse decided to come close. They were too darned close already. Then two riders detached themselves and rode toward us, touching their hats and saying hullo. I sprang into the jeep so quickly I almost knocked out Marcia who was frantically scrambling in on the other side. We both shouted, "Please go away!" to the riders, then looked at each other and roared with laughter—she was scared too. A great bond!

Beagling held no such terrors for me, the largest animal involved being the beagles themselves. In England, it was a sport that satisfied my husband completely. This is how he describes it.

Following beagles—or their ancestors, hounds that look rather more like an English "long dog"—on foot, was a favorite sport in ancient Greece. Even earlier civilizations had fostered the sport and, certainly for the last thousand years, the English have been particularly addicted to it.

In the centuries during which hunting deer, the followers usually mounted, was a royal prerogative, it is possible that the pursuit of the humble hare, with smaller hounds, was permitted amongst the lower orders.

Something of the same idea has been perpetuated in England to this day. People who like to hunt, but don't ride or can't afford to keep a horse and all the paraphernalia of fox hunting, are apt to go beagling instead. It is arguable that a member of the field sees far more sport, more hound work with beagles. The cost is negligible; strangers are welcome and invited to put a few shillings into the cap at the meet.

"Whipping-in" to a pack of beagles is strenuous sport but great fun. It is particularly rewarding when the whips, alone perhaps with the huntsman, find that they have covered so much ground so fast that they are alone with hounds at a kill, or at the end of a day's sport.

But it is not the object of the exercise to shake off the field, a heterogeneous collection of men, women, and children who follow, in tough old clothes that will not suffer unduly from scrambling through thick hedges, over barbed wire fences, across deep, wet plough and occasionally through streams. Older members of the field learn to anticipate the movements of the hare. For instance, a hunted hare that starts bearing to the left usually continues in that direction; so the veterans cut corners and make for a convenient rise in the ground from which they can watch the sport without exhausting themselves. The younger members of the field, like the whips, try to keep up with the pack, and enjoy coming somewhere near to the point of exhaustion in the process.

A pack of beagles is not so fast that it is impossible to keep them in sight in open country. Beagles cannot go as fast as a hare, when it is fresh; but, by nature (preserved in the breeding), they have good "noses" and great staying power. So, theoretically, the pack eventually runs down its quarry and there is a kill, instantaneous, usually, since the leading hound nips the hare at the base of the neck.

But the vagaries of scent, the inborn wiles of the hare, and the hazards of the countryside all combine to save most hares that are hunted, giving them little more than a stretch (a little exercise, twice a week, that keeps them in condition). Hunting also encourages hares to resort to their natural cunning in avoiding capture. Puss will double back along her "line," then make a tremendous jump sideways, thus throwing hounds off the scent. She will swim a stream, run through a flock of sheep, and adopt a host of subterfuges, all designed to confuse her pursuers. More than once I have seen a hunted hare push up a fresh hare, found resting in her form, "clamp down" herself, and watch hounds streak after their new quarry, which they have little chance of catching for hours.

Depending, therefore, upon conditions, upon the skill of the huntsman in assisting and encouraging his hounds (he should not interfere too much) and, most of all, upon that elusive factor, scent, a day's hunting with beagles might be long and strenuous, with hardly a pause for breath before a fresh hare gets up and hounds go racing after her, or comparatively dull and tedious. Sometimes there is little or no action beyond a long walk, whilst the pack searches in vain or fails to own the "line" of the hare for more than a couple of fields.

But beaglers—regulars, that is—take the rough with the smooth and accept the uncertainties of the sport. The chance that even the most unlikely-looking day might go down in the annals as a red-letter day is part of the fun of it.

To the uninitiated all this might sound very peculiar: a strange way of enjoying oneself. Simple bucolic joys? Perhaps, but the pleasures of beagling are both physical and aesthetic. There is something about the sight and sound of it all; about being out of doors in winter, when the countryside is deserted and a frieze of bare trees against the skyline looks particularly beautiful, that exercises a strange fascination; and the more one does it the more one enjoys it. The exhilaration that comes from all that running, all that fresh air, and scrambling over rough country, through hedges and ditches, often getting wet and scratched as well as physically tired, has to be experienced to be believed.

Strenuous physical endeavor, in contact with the elements, in the company of a few kindred spirits, has a strong, traditional hold upon many Englishmen, especially those born and raised in the country. The enjoyment of the countryside is enhanced by participating in it, as distinct from merely looking at it, passively. There is some satisfaction, too, in following a sport that survives unchanged, serves to keep the hare population within reasonable bounds, and has provided fun, fresh air, and exercise for generations of Englishmen. At the very least, a Saturday spent in this manner provides a welcome contrast and antidote to the weekly round of sedentary, soft, and, usually, far too comfortable living in the town. Or so I have found for most of my life.

We had never seen beagles treated as pets before we came to America; in England they are always working dogs and we were all surprised to see them in the backs of cars, looking perfectly happy, although usually overfed, as part of the family. Teddy had, from early youth, followed beagles and was whipping in to the Aldershot Command Beagles when I first met him.

There are, of course, in England as well as in America, thousands of young men whose idea of exercise is to sit in a grandstand watching a few energetic fellows kicking a ball around. But I do think that more young men in England continue to take strenuous exercise. Anyway, they are always off playing rugby or hockey or walking or beagling. Beagling was Edward's favorite sport and, when I first met him, rain or shine, all through the autumn and winter, off he would go beagling on Saturday. I said "when I first met him" but I was never able to change this habit and he continued to do it, with a break for the war of course, until he came to America. If I wanted to be with Teddy on a Saturday, before and after we were married, I would have to don slacks and heavy shoes and be prepared to drive with him to the meet. This would be held anywhere within a radius of seventy miles, at a country house or village pub, and always a small glass of sherry or cherry brandy would be served to fortify these hardy souls for the exacting day ahead. Lunch was nonexistent; it was considered sissy to have anything more than an apple in your pocket. We would set off at 11 A.M. and continue until 4:30 when hounds would be called off, unless they happened to be running well at that time. After the hunt a member would provide tea, usually boiled eggs and brown bread and butter, cut very thin, and delicious dark fruit cake.

This is a lovely memory. A beautiful English country house, the way one's skin felt, the glorious feeling of relaxation after the long day out of doors, the chat about the day's hunting, and then the drive home.

I usually did this and I enjoyed it, but sometimes I would think that perhaps we could do this or that on Saturday instead. But no; Teddy was adamant; if there was beagling, he beagled. I will admit that one of the first things I secretly thought when he told me we were coming to live in America for two years was "Jolly good, no beagling." But, do you know? Within four days of my arrival here, I found myself beagling on Long Island. There were slight differences; they met on Sunday afternoon and ran for a shorter time. But the people were the same except for their accents *and* we had tea at a lovely country house. The only thing that struck me as odd was that at one end of the long dining room table sat a lady dispensing tea in a silver pot, as in England, but at the other end sat another lady dispensing coffee. Coffee? At tea time?

Walking in America was another matter. It was possible to walk if one drove many miles to a place like Pound Ridge, and this we sometimes did. But it was impossible to go for a shorter brisk walk close to home. There were no footpaths and too many cars offering one lifts, or splashing one from head to toe. I had already had experience of the difficulty of walking anywhere when I had tried to walk to school with Charles, but Teddy refused to learn his lesson.

As I have said before, he had always been a great walker, and one soon learned to do the sensible thing and sit and enjoy the view until he came back, rather than have him behave like a hunter on a tight rein, obviously holding himself in check to match one's puny efforts. He is a tall man and he would charge along at a terrific pace. Many's the man I have seen fall by the wayside; men who regarded themselves as reasonably fit and who were fond of walking would make feeble excuses the second time they were asked. There is one story which illustrates this point, told to me by an old friend of Teddy's.

The first holiday in the year in England is the long week end at Easter, which includes Good Friday, Saturday, Easter Sunday and Easter Monday. As the weather is often pretty unsettled at that time of the year, walking (when you're young) is the great activity. Teddy persuaded two friends to join him in a walk around the Isle of Wight: a distance of approximately sixty-five miles.

The Isle of Wight is a lovely island off the South Coast of England, which many Americans will have seen when they sail into Southampton in one of the ocean liners. There are beautiful beaches, cliffs, and farmland. The three young men set off, bursting with energy.

The first day was fine and, when they settled into their feather beds in a farmhouse that night, they were all looking forward to the next day's stint. By the second night one young man was feeling just a wee bit ragged; he fell into bed in a stupor; but the second young man was game to walk to the top of a neighboring hill with Teddy after dinner "to get a breath of fresh air."

On the third day the second young man was also beginning to look for somewhere peaceful to rest his weary bones, but the only respite they had was when Number One found he had a blister on his heel and Teddy made them climb down a cliff to the sea so that the young man could soak his feet, salt water being the best cure for blisters. Teddy had a brisk swim in the cold water and off they straggled again.

On the fourth day they had encircled the island and were in view of Ryde pier, where they were to catch the ferry back to the mainland.

They stood on a stone wall, I was told, and surveyed the landscape. Then Teddy said, "Come along, we must get moving if we want to catch the next ferry." He jumped off the wall, landed on a small rock, spraining his ankle, and lay on the ground unable to move. "We just," said the other young man, "had the strength to raise a faint cheer."

One very wet day in Connecticut, feeling pent up, Teddy decided to walk along the byroads. He thought there would be little traffic as it was pouring with rain. For a while he was able to stride along happily, but first one car and then another would stop and offer him a lift. He refused many times, but, when he realized he was being offered a lift for the third time by the same people in the same car, he began to feel hunted. He cut down another side road and found himself standing at the entrance to a house. It was still raining. In the picture window of the house he could see a man, reading a newspaper, who looked up when he became aware of my husband standing there trying to get his bearings. The man leaped up, knocked at the window, and made signs for my husband to wait. He next appeared backing out of his garage in a new Cadillac. He came alongside my husband and said, "Jump in, Commander. I'll drive you home." The Commander jumped in and looked at his savior, who was chewing a big black cigar. He looked vaguely familiar so Teddy said diffidently, "Er—haven't we met?" "Why, yes," said the man, "I am your garbage collector."

CHAPTER 16

AS time went on I was still husbandless lots of the time, although we were now at least in the same hemisphere as Edward.

Although life on the small island was simple, life itself was becoming very complicated. I spent an incredible amount of time meeting Edward off 'planes from Canada, Mexico, Venezuela, the Caribbean, dashing to New York, dashing back to the country. Answering the telephone to someone who wanted to know the Schweppes story. Would Commander Whitehead do this, that, or the other? I was, as all wives are to a certain extent, the unpaid curate. There were requests for Edward's attendance at all sorts of functions.

He was asked to give the sermon in a church. "We are sure," he was told, "that you will have the opportunity to mention Schweppes." However dedicated, he could not bring himself to be that commercial.

Speaking at men's business luncheons or conferences he regarded as a definite and important part of his business, and this took up a lot of his time. He enjoyed making speeches, as he also enjoyed being interviewed by an intelligent person. It seems that once one is prominent, for any reason, one's views are sought on any subject under the sun, and one usually gives them. Since Edward is articulate and has views on a wide range of subjects, particularly anything to do with Britain and the British, and the extent to which they are misunderstood in the United States—and vice versa—it gave him terrific satisfaction to encourage people to think differently. Even in so small a matter as the British—particularly the English—being pompous and having no sense of humor. All this of course became more significant as he began to penetrate into the parts of America where even interviewers hadn't met an Englishman before. I was beginning to think of Edward as a one-man task force fighting the battle of the British Empire all over again. And the people who were giving him most help were Americans: the very people whose land he was hoping to take over for his company. During interviews, Edward never mentioned his product uninvited; his interviewers usually did it for him, most generously, until eventually in some quarters Edward, the British Empire, and Schweppes became synonymous.

There were some requests which, when inadvertently acceded to, made poor Edward feel as out of place, as he delicately put it, as "a whore at a christening." And this brings up the subject of public relations, which, as we all know, is completely separate from advertising.

The purpose of advertising, which is to introduce the product to the public and present it in the best possible light so that everyone gallops out to buy it, is definite and clear.

But Public Relations—the nurturing of the image that springs to mind when a product or person is mentioned—is much more subtle.

There was Edward with the whole Public Relations image of his Company wrapped up in himself. Public Relations was not exactly new to him of course. His Treasury job had had a large Public Relations ingredient, but there are differences in attitudes in America. It was sometimes difficult for Edward to convince a really keen PR type that complete obscurity was preferable to bad publicity. That however much Schweppes the hotel, or chain, or whatever, used, he wasn't going to be photographed with his arm around a bathing belle, or even with a bevy of belles, which he had allowed to happen once, thinking there was a certain amount of security in admiring girls *en masse*. To Edward's mortification, this picture was printed in the *London Evening Standard*. ("Gad! Whitehead is really letting the side down!")—and induced my mother to write us a letter asking, "What was *I* doing!"

Nor, said Edward, was he going to sit in a television studio at 11 A.M. so that the star of the show could say, "Look who we have in our audience today" and invite him before the cameras for a chat. "What sort of businessman would people think me," said Edward, "if I appear to spend my mornings in a studio moronically clapping my hands when someone holds up a card saying, 'Applaud' when I should be in my office running my business?"

Neither, said Edward, would he normally kiss an airline hostess, however pretty, after a flight, nor would he allow anyone to be photographed pulling his beard for luck or any other reason. None of these things would do anything to enhance the standing of his company in the United States. Finally, neither would he endorse anyone else's product although offers of large sums of money to do so were numerous.

The only time I have known Edward willing to help with the testing of another product was when a rather sad little man who was hoping to promote a new fishing line appeared at the side of a large swimming pool where Edward was the only person swimming. Naturally! The little man, who had arrived with a photographer, had apparently expected to find dozens of people in the pool, all of whom would be glad to wear a harness to which the line would be fastened. The little man would stand at the edge of the pool playing his human fish with a very light rod.

Would Edward help? Edward, realizing that his face would be hidden in the water and feeling sorry for the sad little man, agreed. The experiment didn't last long. Everything was set, photographer in position, Edward swam away, the sad little man let the line out, then reeled it in.

It broke at once and the sad little man fell backwards onto the flagstones, receiving a slight concussion. Edward was full of compassion for him and wished he had swum less strongly.

Edward's approach to the subject of Public Relations is,

it must be obvious, the reverse of the slick, slightly bogus, "front building" operation usually judged by quantitative results, column inches in the press, and/or time on TV and radio that sometimes passes for Public Relations.

In speeches and writing he has often stated his own Public Relations policy as: 1. Losing no legitimate opportunity to focus *desirable* attention on the merits of his company and its products. 2. Preserving a decent reticence.

The second, he says, does not in fact preclude the first. He maintains his position by refusing to do anything he regards as out of character, though this has sometimes caused bafflement among the Public Relations people involved who still could not understand why there should be any such limitations.

As far as Edward was concerned, if, after having met and talked to a PR man, that same man suggested that Edward should join a jolly party going to Coney Island where he could be photographed eating one of those enormous hot dogs, the insensitive fellow would be dropped. Not that Edward has a thing against the people who go to Coney Island, but it is far removed from his idea of fun, and hot dogs he simply loathes, though he has never in fact eaten one. Edward felt he was making quite enough of a poppy show of himself appearing in the advertising. Any other kind of publicity should at least present him as he really is, even if it isn't madly exciting to the publicity hounds. Incidentally, while Edward found that he did meet an occasional PR man who was *sympatico*, the odds against it were so long that Edward preferred to conduct his own affairs without their professional assistance. It has been a matter of constant surprise to him that there has been no decline in the number of requests to appear or speak, despite the fact that he is only able to accept about one in ten.

Not that he would want to knock Public Relations, but there is a world of difference between building a false façade

—"Say what you like as long as you spell my name right"—and Edward's favorite definition, "earned recognition."

The fact is that this had happened to a man who is by nature rather serious, whose idea of bliss after a week of hard work (never a slacker, our Edward) is to commune with nature during the day, alone or with a congenial companion —never a crowd—and then to spend his evenings writing and listening to music. So, much as Edward liked meeting people, which he would have done anyway in the course of his labors, it was hard to have to put on a public face and wear it even when he didn't feel like it.

As for me, I am eternally grateful that we had had that short and at least partly anonymous period when we could travel America and do all the simple things without being accosted by someone who would want to know if this was the guy on TV. True, we were sometimes eyed as though we were creatures from outer space but once it was established that we were English, all was understood and presumably forgiven. Also, we had been doing some studying of the local inhabitants ourselves, and we found them just as interesting and curious. The crew cut was in its heyday. Man and boy sported this form of singularly unbecoming haircut, regardless of the shape of the head. The crew cut is just possible if a young man has a good round head and thick dark hair. We sometimes intercepted amused glances induced, we realized, by the hirsute appearance of the male members of my family, Teddy's beard and Charles's English non-haircut—and probably, now I come to think of it, my own hairdo, which bordered on the bird's nest. The smiles were often on the lips of young men or boys, who sported no hair at all. Strange, we thought.

Still, we didn't know them and they didn't know us and we could laugh at each other and sometimes talk to each other; it is one of the most rewarding things to talk to a complete stranger whom you will never see again, who will never be able to check on your flights of fancy—much better than psychoanalysis.

I was doing America, delighted with everything I saw, but the pall of recognition that hung over our lives made one yearn for the end of our two years and London where Edward would be a man with a beard, not *the* man with *the* beard. Which object, I hasten to say before it occurs to someone else to do so, we never once thought of removing, feeling such an act would be weak and an admission of defeat.

Anyway, we are *fond* of it.

CHAPTER 17

BEFORE our two-year period in the United States was ended a big decision was made that affected our lives considerably. Instead of returning to our own country we would stay in America for an indefinite period. Instead of resuming control of the rest of the world at large, with headquarters in London, Edward would continue to concentrate on North America.

His early predictions had proved to be correct and his exchange of hemisphere-hopping for globe-trotting had resulted in success for his company. His personal influence was in no way diminished; on the contrary, it was stronger than ever and there were enormous tracts of un-Schweppt country just waiting to be taken over.

The bottlers (a lovely name which conjures up in my mind a picture of rows of jolly men sitting in a pub called The Jolly Bottler) were the most important people in Edward's business. Since Schweppes had no plants in the United States, the bottling had to be done by franchise arrangements. All Edward wanted was the very best bottler in any area and of course he got him, as all our bottling chums will agree. Edward by this time had something of a reputation as a speaker, and his success in that field did a lot to endear him to the franchisees (there *can't* be such a word!) who were no less alive to the value of the publicity stemming from a successful speech made in their particular area.

As the number of bottlers increased, covering the country more thoroughly, there were profits to be ploughed back into the business, enhancing the margin provided for advertising. The business was booming and it would be utter madness to abandon this fertile field, which Edward was cultivating so successfully, not only in terms of free publicity but also in his management of the business.

Over and above all this, he had grown to like America and Americans. He enjoyed living and working in an expansionist atmosphere; it suited his temperament. He was putting into practice the theories of his Treasury days. He found that American businessmen really do believe in competition, that fierce rivalry in the market place has the end result of expanding the total market, providing a larger cake to be divided among the contestants. His chief rivals were helpful and encouraging and the fact that Edward's efforts were going to expand the market for a virtually new product and that all would share in the benefits was tacitly understood. This detracted neither from the keenness of the competition nor from appreciation, on Edward's part, of the constructive attitude of his rivals.

There was no apparent resentment against a foreign interloper in a business that had until then been the exclusive perquisite of a few domestic companies.

When one comes to think about it, why should there be? Trade has to be international and a few American companies had long since made their products household names in England. I am thinking particularly at this moment of Kellogg's Cornflakes, which invaded the British breakfast table ousting the good old oatmeal porridge, and Bird's who produced custard powder, which the British embraced with such fervor that every pudding is smothered in it and which has contributed a lot to wrecking Britain's reputation in the culinary world.

I could appreciate the business reasons for staying but there were other considerations that affected us both. England was home. We had enjoyed our life there. In England we had family and close friends—old friends with whom we could relax. Our face muscles were beginning to hurt from smiling constantly. Being smiled at was becoming tedious too. We yearned for the sight of a bad-tempered, slightly contemptuous English face. It would be a relief to be able to grumble about the government and curse about the weather.

Truly it is difficult always living in someone else's country. One cannot criticize because one might be told "all right, if you don't like it why don't you go home?" so one resists the temptation, which makes for very dull conversation.

It will be noted that the life of a businessman and his family is not all fat expense accounts and gay trips across the Atlantic.

We had to face the prospect of being cut off from the important things in family life, such as births and marriages and deaths, unless they could be arranged to coincide with our visits home. Transatlantic jets would get us there in hours but ailing parents, for instance, knowing the cost, would forbear to demand our presence until, alas, too late.

For me, the biggest wrench was the separation from Jacq and her family, which had now been increased by the addition of a son. When we received the cable announcing that Jason had been born, Charles, who was now an uncle for the second time at the age of seven, was at first delighted, then his face crumpled and he left the room. "How could Jacq give the baby such a horrible name," he asked. "Why couldn't she have named him Red or something?" (This was the result of too much Roy Rogers.) I pointed out that he could call the new baby Jake, and this is what he did. After all, how could you possibly be uncle to anyone with such a dude name as Jason when you were, if not the fastest, at least the most heavily loaded, gun on the Island? When about eighteen months later my daughter had her second son and called him Jasper, Charles had accepted and secretly rather admired this nonconformism in his sister's choice of names. But when one day we were looking at a house which bore a notice saying

Amos Cooper   1685

he said, "Don't let's tell Jacq about it. She'll have another baby just to give it that name."

Charles's education was another matter. Had we stayed in

120

England he would have gone to boarding school at the age of eight. I have discussed this aspect of English education with many Americans who think it is too early to send boys away from home, and I am in complete agreement with them. Obviously, in England, this custom became a necessity when our pillars of Empire found themselves thousands of miles from home with no decent schools, and their little boys getting a bit beyond Amahs and Nannies and Governesses. Also, as those in Government usually moved to a new country every two years or so they probably felt that their children would have a more settled existence at school. The idea spread to include boys whose parents lived permanently in Britain.

We considered sending Charles to England to school, and flying him backward and forward across the Atlantic for holidays, but, hooray, we decided he was much too young, so he stayed with us until he was thirteen: a decision we have never regretted. In defiance of gloomy warnings of British acquaintances who assured us that educated Charles would not be in America and we'd be sorry, I was delighted to be spared the early parting from our son. This was the sweetener that helped me swallow the pill. And pill it was. In spite of the fact that I had enjoyed being in America there were things in England, personal things, that belonged only to me.

However, I would not like to give the impression that I stayed in America against my will. Before the decision was made I was consulted all along the line in a most flattering fashion and was cleverly made to feel that the fortunes of Schweppes, British Exports, and possibly American-Anglo relations would be destroyed if I made the wrong decision. Not that the feeling lasted—in fact, I always did suspect that I was being hornswoggled but the flattery was quite irresistible.

We felt we could not have "roots" in a rented house so we left our seashore house and bought another, deeper into Connecticut, and proceeded to try to live in America as though we belonged, instead of as visitors.

CHAPTER 18

HAVING made the decision to stay in America we had to reconcile ourselves to the idea of Edward's continuing his dual role of running the Company and modeling on the side, but only, we kept telling ourselves, until a better idea for promoting his product was advanced.

One of the things that had made me want to go back to England was the unwelcome attentions of amateur photographers. In Florida, for instance, we would find ourselves a stretch of beach and settle down with our books. We would watch the hermit crabs scuttling away and the little sandpipers running eternally up and down the shore never getting their feet wet, as the long waves broke slowly over the silver sand. We would watch the pelicans flap ludicrously into the air, then soar with all the ease and grace of gulls.

Then our peace would be shattered. A man and woman would appear walking along the beach. The man, wearing one of those ghastly droopy bathing shorts with a natty matching coat, would be festooned with cameras and light meters. As they drew near there'd be a halt, a whispered conversation, then the lady would detach herself and saunter nonchalantly behind us. We would keep our eyes glued to our books. The gentleman would fiddle with his camera, then he too would amble toward us. As he got within range we'd become aware of heavy breathing very close to our ears and there would be the lady wearing a bright smile being photographed with her head leaning coyly toward Edward's ear.

An alternative to this was for someone to approach our table when we were having lunch outside. A shadow would fall over our plates, we would look up to see a small group arranging itself for posterity around us. The camera would click just as I'd be taking a large bite out of one of those impossible-to-cope-with sandwiches decorated with tooth-picks.

Then there was the man who wasted a considerable amount of time trying to get a picture of Edward drinking a rival product. He spent a whole evening maneuvering, apparently under the impression that we were unaware that anything was going on. We were sitting at a table in a very smart res-taurant. We had been there before and we knew that it wasn't normal to move furniture around during dinner. We ate the delicious food, but our faces were becoming just a little bit stony. Chat was definitely meager. We were *aware*. When a photographer appeared, heaven knows where from, the maneuvering gentleman quickly raised the opened rival bottle of "fizz" and placed it before my husband. Guess whose white crepe dress was drenched in fizzy water! What was intended as a not very funny joke ended in apologies as I made my way to the powder room. I was cast down for a long time; white crepe is *so* very difficult to keep fresh.

There was the woman who planted her baby in Edward's lap, stepped back and took a picture. Teddy was a little wor-ried about the possible repercussions of that one but there was nothing he could do but look fatuous. He couldn't drop the baby—it was rather sweet—neither could he break the camera—far too melodramatic. However, we heard nothing further so perhaps the picture didn't come out.

The most maddening amateur photographer to me was the man at San Juan airport who, spotting Edward at the ticket counter, insisted on showing me how to work his camera, draped his overnight bag over my shoulder, then going up to Edward, turned him round to face me, put his arm round his shoulders and ordered me to "O.K. Shoot." I could kick myself for meekly obeying him, especially as he collected his belongings and went off with an airy wave of the hand and never a thank you.

There have been dozens of charming strangers who have

said "Commander, would you mind—" and Commander has been delighted to comply though he sometimes feels he should *at least* allow himself to be shot into outer space to justify the attention he receives.

Then there was the strange world of the professional photographer and professional model to which Edward was introduced. He found that the popular idea that male models are narcissistic deviates is erroneous, most of them being conscientious and hard-working at modeling and usually another vocation or avocation as well. He found them as normal and moral as the next man. One of New York's most popular male models who appeared in an early Schweppes advertisement spent all his time writing plays when not before the cameras, keeping his ribs apart. And he later had one produced on Broadway.

As for the girls, Edward confirmed my opinion, based on my own early experience, that while it is reasonable to suppose that some had interesting relationships with a photographer or a key executive in an agency, these were no more frequent or obvious than similar relationships in any other profession. A beautiful model had far more to lose if she began every day with dark circles under her eyes, so she'd be much more likely to be strong in resisting the blandishments of the predatory male. Edward, who claims that he admires intelligent women, was sometimes disappointed that, generally speaking, the girl models' intellect and conversational powers did not come up to the standard of their physical beauty. But if you're twenty and that gorgeous, who cares?

Edward positively loathed being photographed in a studio. He always throws open the windows of any room he enters. We had often had battles in railway carriages with other unfortunate travelers who objected to a blast of air blowing their newspapers or veils or hair about the place. This didn't happen so much in England, of course, because most Englishmen seem to feel they will die of suffocation in ten minutes unless there is a good cross draft.

So the heated studio, with powerful lights sending the temperature up even higher, was torture. In one of the early photographs Teddy had to wear a heavy duffle coat, hold a drink in his hand, and look rugged, while someone sprinkled artificial snow over him in an unbearably high temperature. As he had walked to the studio a small blizzard raged in New York, so when he realized they were trying to create the same effect inside, he said, "I shall expire if I stay here—let's take the pictures outside." Richard Avedon said, "Of course that's the thing—let's go up on the roof." They trooped up and got a simply marvelous picture with Teddy looking really happy instead of limp.

Fortunately the people who worked with Teddy in this soon got his wave length and generally outdoor situations would be dreamed up, so that they could be sure of getting him to stay in front of the camera.

Another thing that made Edward feel rather pinched in the early days was the number of people who turned up for a photographic session, be it for a television commercial or a still photograph.

He'd count the number of people standing around and ask if they were spectators, in which case he wished they'd go away, or otherwise what were they contributing? He learned that for each man doing a definite job there were usually several whose jobs were difficult to define. All day they would sit around smoking, using up all the air (the hardest cross for Teddy to bear) and getting at the sandwiches and drinks first when a break was announced.

There were times when Edward (the unwilling nonmethod actor) would have to try to gaze interestedly at a girl model, but his mind would be busily totting up the possible combined salaries of the thirty-five people present and wondering how much this was going to add to the costs. A *very* definite snag—being president and model.

As time went on he learned to accept the fact that there are some things that cannot be changed and it is a waste of time trying; and if the unions require that a special "prop" man has to stand around all day to move one small bottle from A to B, well, so be it!

It was undoubtedly difficult both for photographers and producers and agency people to cope with a model who had ideas of his own. Edward, who is of the opinion that one should not keep a dog and bark oneself, tried to suppress his critical faculty and his own ideas to the point that he was not questioning every move in the game. But he could never swallow flagrantly wasteful procedures nor anything inappropriate, or out of character for himself or his Company. That subtle something that gave Schweppes advertisements their special character had to be carefully preserved and nurtured.

For my part I have to confess to having brought down the wrath of David Ogilvy on my unrepentant head by criticizing, rather late in the day, a photograph for an advertisement almost ready to appear, causing much backtracking and retaking. One might imagine that given good lights, a good camera, a good idea, and Edward, it would be impossible to produce a bad photograph, but it has happened. The photograph I objected to had captured Teddy looking like Charles Laughton doing the Twist while sitting on a stool. Most peculiar. Edward, perhaps feeling that the concept of the advertisement was more important than the way he looked in it, had accepted the best of a bad lot. But not I. Just as Edward demanded the best for Schweppes I demanded the best for Edward. If I was consulted, that is. I can't think why I wasn't always shown the pictures before the advertisement was a *fait accompli!*

One disturbing thing my husband had discovered early on was that, in the East especially, after Labor Day, gin and Tonic was dropped and Scotch, Martinis or Bourbon took its place. This seemed to be the established pattern. It was autumn, so one needed something to keep the cold out;

although the temperature stayed up in the eighties. This was the way people thought. The sun that used never to set on the British Empire now shines down constantly somewhere in the United States, so there is always a market open for long thirst-quenching drinks. But Edward wanted to eradicate the impression that his product could not become the year-round drink it is in Britain. It was with this in mind that it was decided to have some pictures taken at a skiing area.

I heard about the proposed trip only a day or so before they were actually going, but when I did I insisted upon joining them, with Charles. Everyone concerned was surprised. Many other photographs had been taken by this time, some with beautiful girls on beaches, or at swimming pools, and I had expressed no desire at all to be present. (Naturally, I had been *interested*, but I had been hoping that if I took no notice it would go away.) But now they were going to a skiing place. Stowe. I had read about Stowe, and Charles and I were not going to be left behind. Everyone had to change seats or reservations, and off we went. Teddy didn't even have time to make his usual remark that it was useless for me to go as I couldn't ski.

I have no doubt that we would have skied eventually in America because the sport has boomed so much in the time we have been here. But I shall bless forever the photographic session that gave me a start.

We stayed at the Inn at Smugglers Notch. The landscape was completely snow-covered. There was Mount Mansfield with its criss-crossing trails. We were in heaven. I love the snow and when the first flurries appear I get a terrrific feeling of excitement. I have been told by my mother that when I was born, in November, in Wales, her nurse raised the blinds at five o'clock in the morning to find that the garden was deep in snow, a most unusual sight in that part of the world. So she held me in her arms and I gazed upon the outside world. Perhaps, this first picture etched on the mind of a newborn baby has made me love the snow ever since.

Teddy had ski clothes, but Charles and I had no time to get any before we left. Anyway, much as I loved the snow, I wasn't sure that I was going to be able to ski so I didn't want to get all the equipment at that point.

We had all the help possible from the people in charge at Stowe. While the photographic contingent went off looking for likely situations, Charles and I were fitted out and finally taken onto the slopes. In view of the fact that we were launched on our skiing careers by such august members of the skiing world as Sepp Ruscho and Kerr Sparkes, I would love to be able to say that we became expert skiers. Charles is very good and will get better but Teddy and I reached a certain low level of proficiency, and there we stayed. But what we lacked in skill was certainly made up for in enthusiasm, and we like to think we have encouraged many people who thought they were too ancient to ski to take up this, to me, most exhilarating pastime.

The first skiing picture was to be taken at the top of Mt. Mansfield with a glorious background of ice-encased bare branches and heavily snow-laden Christmas trees. For Edward this was fine. He could survey the landscape and breathe in the frosty air, but just as he got into position, feeling somewhat unsteady after twenty years off skis, he heard a voice saying, "Teddy! How lovely to see you. I didn't know you skied." A neighbor of ours in London, who had to be told that Teddy was "working" and as the cameras were icing up would she please move aside. She stood around and watched for a while and later in London we heard that "Poor Teddy must be finding it difficult to make ends meet in America. He was modeling ski clothes. Of course, he's a good-looking chap—but it seems rather odd, don't you think?"

For some unknown reason, once my husband had made it clear that he was not interested in run-of-the-mill advertisements the agency went out of their way to produce rather frightening ideas. I think they were hoping to scare him back to beautiful girls and swimming pools, which *must* be much more pleasant subjects; but he was a little anxious about the effect of that kind of thing on his family (though secretly I believe they made him feel rather a dog).

They decided to do an authentic climbing picture, which was to show Teddy roped above and below, on a more or less vertical cliff, hauling up a case of Schweppes to prepare for a "Conference at the Summit" (topical at the time). Not to be outdone in terms of authenticity, the agency had sought out a mountain range not too far from New York. The party set off very early on a cold morning in February. I didn't go but my husband has described the day to me. Somewhere in the Appalachian range they met by arrangement the person who had been described to Teddy as his "anchor man." It was a girl. Attractive, too. She was going to hold the rope somewhere above him and out of sight, so that if he slipped he would not crash to the valley below. He felt it was a little invidious to be held up by a girl. He almost chickened out (if you'll forgive the expression), but her professional skill, her whole approach to the problem, finally won his confidence.

The worst feature of that expedition was the intense cold, some 25 degrees below freezing, and the time it took to capture the episode on film. It took the photographer a couple of hours to get himself secured, with pitons, on a convenient ledge, once the exact location for the picture had been decided. Meanwhile, Teddy was clinging to the face of the cliff, rapidly losing interest and any vestige of enthusiasm for this particular project. He has always held that it is much easier to be brave when warm. Cold saps the very stuff of courage, he says, physical or moral. When the last picture was taken and he found himself on level ground again he wondered why he had allowed himself to get into such a situation. Well, some people climb Everest or sail the Atlantic single-handed for the honor and glory of their country. While others find themselves literally hanging off the Schwangunks in an effort to close the trade gap.

It was a little maddening to be asked, when the climbing

advertisement appeared, "Had the picture been taken in a studio with him lying down and then turned the other way up?" If it were not for his passion for versimilitude he could have saved himself a lot of risk, trouble, and discomfort.

The next idea was that he should be photographed in a helicopter with his usual case of Schweppes aboard. He had no qualms this time because seated beside him, piloting the plane and dressed as a chauffeur, was the chief test pilot of Bell Aircraft. The door had to be removed from the helicopter on Teddy's side so that the photographer, flying around in another machine, could get unobstructed pictures when they flew side by side. The photographer was insatiable, he wanted more and more pictures.

Finally Teddy's pilot announced firmly that he was running out of gas and was going down. As they touched down Teddy saw that the petrol gauge indicated that there was still half a tank. Why? he asked. "Because," said the pilot, "it is the most dangerous job I've ever done, and I'm so bloody cold."

When I heard of this little adventure I began to doubt my husband's sanity, especially as this had to be done without insurance. Heavens, one thought, is this modern business? In the old days the British businessman, beating the bushes for world trade, had only simple things like malaria and unfriendly natives to wrestle with. But helicopters with no doors, and rock climbing and no privacy, and hardly any family life? One was moved to burst into poetry. To misquote William Ernest Henley:

> What am I doing for you,
> England my England,
> What is there I would not do,
> England my own?

And I, a Welshwoman!

The inevitable result of these advertisements, combined with press, radio interviews, and television appearances, was that he found it more and more difficult to have a private life. I have met many television people who look only vaguely like themselves off camera. Make-up, which is considered essential for men and women, does have this effect. Teddy wouldn't use make-up unless he had to—after all, where would they put it? So allowing for occasional distortion by the camera, he looked more or less the same off as on.

He was constantly being recognized, and, in the early days, not always as himself. One day, before the first advertisements appeared, Teddy was walking down Park Avenue. He usually walks carrying his hat in his hand, and on this occasion the morning sun, shining through his beard and lighting up his hair, must have cast a glow round him. He became aware of a little old lady walking—almost running—beside him, saying something which he couldn't believe he had heard. But she repeated her question, "Are you Christ?" Teddy staggered across the road into the arms of a waiting policeman who fined him two dollars on the spot for jaywalking.

We were invited by the English Speaking Union to see the film of the South Polar Expedition undertaken by Fuchs. We sat in the darkness and watched and were thrilled by the exploits of this tough band of men. All were bearded, but Fuchs was a tall man with a fairish reddish beard, not unlike Teddy's. When the film was over and we had said thank-you to our hosts there was a sudden, subdued cry. "Here is the great man himself!" Teddy, well aware that his own exploits had not caused the excitement in the bosoms of English Speaking Union Ladies, realized he was being mistaken for Dr. Fuchs. By this time he was surrounded by a large crowd congratulating him and wanting to shake his hand. He didn't have the heart to tell them how wrong they were, so presumably they went to bed happy in the thought that they had met the intrepid explorer. Later we met Dr. Fuchs, who was amused by this incident. He and Teddy thought they might

131

double for each other occasionally. To some people, all bearded men look alike, like the Chinese.

On the opposite end of the scale were the two young men who audibly murmured "Mr. Schweppes" as my husband walked past them at the swimming pool at the Olympic Club in San Francisco. Teddy was a guest of the club so, instead of ignoring the young men as he would have done outside, he turned toward them with a smile. Whereupon one said, "Oh, sorry, sir, for a moment we thought you were the old boy in the Schweppes advertisements."

Ah well, such is fame.

Life was sufficiently complicated being recognized as himself. He found there just wasn't time during the day to stop and talk to strangers who wanted to tell him that they were now Schweppes addicts. He is a very kind and gentle man who hates being rude and rarely loses his temper (only when people won't open windows!) so he had to evolve a technique for getting from A to B. He didn't always want to take a taxi.

In New York his habit is to walk to his office every day, making a detour through Central Park, a distance of forty or more blocks. He walks at a fast pace so that very few can fall in with him. If he meets someone who begins, "Hi, Commander, I," he waves his hand, says good morning, and strides on without faltering. When he gets to a traffic light, he doesn't just stand there, he walks the other way. In fact, he has an instinct for traffic lights such as some taxi drivers have. I wouldn't advise anyone to walk through the New York streets with him. There's never a moment to catch one's breath.

On trains and 'planes when he is alone, he glues himself to his newspaper or his writing, always regarding these enforced, physically inactive periods as heaven-sent opportunities to get some work done. I know how difficult it is to penetrate the wall, because I have sat beside him from New York to California and not a word has been exchanged, though at intervals he does pat me to let me know he knows I am there. I expect it is always like this after long years of marriage. When I see a married couple conversing animatedly together I think they must be quarreling.

Often, of course, Teddy would be with people who were also anxious to be left alone and then a perfectly happy time would be had by all. Sometimes an interesting conversation would develop naturally with a neighbor. But to be trapped in one's seat by a bore is utter torture. It has happened to all of us, but it must be worse for the person who is what is called a celebrity. I remember seeing exactly the same look on Bing Crosby's face, when I entered an elevator of which he was the only occupant, that Teddy wears when he thinks some ghastly woman is going to say things to him. So I know.

If the celebrity, man or woman, is a kind person, he cannot brush people off. Anyway, in Teddy's case, rudeness would probably ruin his business. But it must be awfully hard work to be "on stage" all the time, and Teddy had the added difficulty of not believing there was any reason why people should consider him a celebrity or want to gossip with him. He was a business man. Period. And he was no Paul Getty.

Apropos of this business of encroachment on privacy, here is an incident that illustrates it.

Whenever possible Teddy would go to his club in New York and swim at lunch time. This was all part of the keep-fit campaign. He could do this easily in an hour. His secretary would call the club and order his lunch. Teddy would walk smartly from his office, swim several lengths of the pool, dry himself, and be ready just as his sandwich appeared. He would then sit, in a small section of the swimming pool area reserved for this purpose, open his *Times,* and begin eating. Very few members used the pool at that time of the day, but some days there was one other man doing exactly the same thing. They ploughed up and down the pool past each other for months, then came out and sat at tables only feet apart in an otherwise deserted room.

They recognized each other's existence with a nod, then buried their noses in their newspapers. Teddy knew very well who this man was. He was an actor whom we had always admired. We had never missed one of his plays or revues and, on television, he was certainly the best Captain Hook it is possible to imagine. We were possibly his oldest fans and had in fact been introduced to him in London. But, Teddy said, they were both wearing their fences. The fact that they were being so pompous wearing very little else, as is the habit when swimming at men's clubs, I understand, made it even more ridiculous.

Ultimately, they met again at a party. On being introduced by their host they both confessed to having known each other for years and to meeting almost daily. They discussed the affairs of the world and enjoyed each other's company. But next time at the club, they nodded and buried their noses in their newspapers. Cyril Ritchard is Australian born, and has lived many years in England, so he knows the rules. As he said, with any other nationality they'd either have been bosom pals or bitter enemies in the time they had met swimming—or one or the other of them would have resigned from the club.

Naturally, when Teddy has to make a speech anywhere he is delighted to meet as many people as possible. He could not have continued with what he is doing if he didn't get some pleasure out of this part of it. Even without the participation in the advertising, he'd have had to go to all parts of America and whip up some enthusiasm. Because of the publicity he had received, he found the people he had to talk to were already interested in meeting him, hearing what he had to say, and most important, becoming intrigued with his product. But I think it is entirely to Teddy's credit, and no one else's, that he had been able to sustain that interest for twelve years with little, if any, help from publicity agents:

none from writers, campaign managers, and all the paraphernalia of men who are constantly before the public eye.

The people call out, "Hi, Mr. Schweppes" or "Hi, Commander" as we drive along the Connecticut Turnpike are
rather fun unless one has the misfortune to get stuck alongside them in a traffic block, but it becomes less than funny
when a Volkswagen full of girls buzzes up alongside one and
stays there for ages, doing seventy, with all heads, including
the driver's, turned in our direction. We try to drop back or
go forward or change lanes, anything to get away from the
dangerous missile swerving toward us, but it is often impossible. We have to stay where we are. Teddy is usually driving
so he is preoccupied and looking ahead, but I find myself
wondering what to do. Should I bow graciously like the
Queen and wave them on? It wouldn't do any good—anyway
they aren't looking at me—so we have to take it until a more
powerful car hoots madly at them from behind and they have
to pull in. We seize the opportunity to get away, but soon,
we hear the distinctive noise of a Volkswagen coming up
again, and then we're being inspected on the other side. A
wave of the hand and a pleasant Hi! is one thing, but being
tailed is one of the worse penalties of identification. Sometimes, desperation sets in.

Talking of tailing, we were driving along the Merritt Parkway one day, quite innocently, doing no more than the lawful
speed limit. A police car appeared behind us, then pulled out
and flagged us down. While we waited in our car for the
policeman to come over to us, we wondered what law we had
broken. We could think of nothing. The policeman asked for
my husband's driving license, and when he had studied it
he said, "Good, I *thought* it was you, Commander. I'd like to
shake your hand." We were so pleased to find we hadn't committed any crime we forgot to be mad.

There have been many instances of recognition in ridiculous or unexpected circumstances.

In our early days Teddy and I were driving back to Connecticut from Canada when we came to the sign which said Whiteface Mountain. We had time in hand so we decided to explore and drove up the road that sweeps around the mountainside, affording the most glorious views of lakes, tree-covered slopes, and jagged, towering rocks. When we got to the place where we could park the car, near the top, we found there was an elevator built inside the mountain to take people up the final bit, which was steep and somewhat rugged. I noticed Teddy studying the terrain. He found a narrow rocky path leading to the top, so he began climbing, having said something about needing the exercise after sitting in the car—as though it was necessary to explain.

I seriously considered using the elevator—there were several people around waiting to go up—but game as ever, I decided to climb too. As I reached the top—it wasn't very far, but it was steep and I was hampered by the fact that I was wearing the car rug wrapped around me like an Indian blanket—the sensible elevator crowd was being disgorged. Teddy, of course, was already there, standing like a statue, looking at the view, on the edge of a small cliff (a sight that always makes me want to lie down or cling to something, even though I am twenty feet away from the edge). "Well," said a man in the crowd, "this must be White*head* Mountain."

Then there was the priest presiding at a funeral who mournfully asked for an autograph as we made our adieus with downcast eyes.

There was the Taj Mahal, glistening in the moonlight—an awe-inspiring sight—and the woman who destroyed the magic by uttering, "Mr. Schweppes I presume?"

There was the time we went *en famille*, to see Pompeii, and then Vesuvius. It was late in the season and there weren't many tourists around. When we got to Vesuvius we were told the chair lift wasn't working because there was too much wind. They didn't know they were talking to a group that had been trained by Edward to spurn any form of transport. We walked up, of course, each of us having been given a white walking stick by our guide. It wasn't pleasant walking cinder paths, with the wind blowing ashes in our faces. Nothing but cinder and ash on the steep sides of the great volcano with, very occasionally, a tiny touch of green, where a minute seedling was struggling to cover the slopes once more with verdant growth.

The Bay of Naples was below us. The sea was so blue, and we went up and up. We reached our first objective and gazed fearfully into the old crater, then continued our climb to a higher spot where the mountain was preparing for its next display of pyrotechnics. Gases poured out of fissures in the ground, there were hissings and bubblings and a strong smell of sulphur. There was no other sound; no birds; no people; nothing moved. We stood transfixed. Then round a bend in the path came a man in a Brooks Brothers suit. "Excuse me, sir," he said. "Aren't you Commander Whitehead?"

To complete our foreign tour we have to go to Paris. I had not been to Montmartre so, late in the season again, Teddy and I went there on a Sunday evening. I don't know why it is that when we hear the word "tourists" we always think of Americans or English. The fact is the British and American tourists had gone home but Montmartre was still crowded with Germans and Scandinavians and even French tourists. We wandered into picture galleries, but we were not tempted to buy anything. We didn't really care for the atmosphere but we didn't want to admit defeat so, when we began to feel hungry, we decided to have dinner at one of the outdoor places in the Square. We were tired after our walk, so we sat quite happily for half an hour looking at the grubby red and white checked tablecloth. A waiter had flashed by several times and finally he gave us a menu. However, he didn't pay any more attention to us for some time. When Teddy managed to hold onto his coat tails, he accepted our order and Teddy chose a bottle of wine. Teddy enjoys wine and likes to see it treated properly and France surely was one country where this would be done. We waited. The wine arrived. Teddy could see it being shaken up as the waiter crossed the road carrying it under his arm. It was planted roughly on the table. No glasses. Another wait. Teddy caught the waiter again, and in Churchillian French made it clear that we were starving. The waiter reached over to the next table and gave us a basket of bread slices. Still no glasses. I ate all the bread. Our first course arrived. Cold, slopped over, onion soup. We helped ourselves to spoons from the next table. The soup, I am dead certain, was made from OXO soaked in tepid water. Teddy suddenly decided we must leave. He stood up, helped me with my coat, and immediately the waiter had all the time in the world to hover over us. Teddy, Churchillian once more, said we were no longer interested in eating. The waiter said, "You must pay for the wine." Teddy said he didn't think even in Montmartre one was expected to drink it out of the bottle. The waiter said, "You've eaten the bread." Teddy said, "Give me a bill and I'll pay for it."

By this time there was a large international crowd around us and considerable noise. Attracted no doubt by all this, a young Charles Boyer type emerged from a nearby house. The owner of the restaurant, who looked at Teddy and said in English, "Commander Whitehead? It's a pleasure to serve you, sir." *Serve?* The waiter was still excited and Teddy had the ignominious task of explaining to the owner that served we had not been.

The owner said, "Please be seated and let me attend to you." We had to explain that after two hours we *really* had lost interest in food. The owner said to the waiter, "Do you know whom you have insulted?" The waiter didn't and he didn't give a damn anyway.

We paid for the bread, tipped the waiter—weak perhaps, but he was a sad little character and we had occupied one of his tables for a long time. It transpired that this particular restaurant was, and still is, we understand, a keen supporter of Schweppes. *Quel horreur!*

There were times when it was particularly maddening to

be recognized. For instance, when learning to ski. Practicing our turns on a slope that was somewhat steeper than we had been led to expect, I would make Teddy go down first and promise to wait for me at a strategic point not too far ahead. He would choose a time when there seemed to be no one behind to crash into us, or whose downhill progress we would impede. He'd do two turns which were very neat, I would shout "Jolly good," and the next turn would just not materialize. We don't know what caused it. Teddy swears it was something to do with having done a lot of riding and developing different muscles for skiing, but he'd find himself with his skis crossed at the back, facing uphill with his face buried in the snow. I never tried to extricate him after the first time, the muffled sounds that emanated from the mêlée being far too ominous. But, as he lay there trying to decide which arm or leg to move first, he would turn his snow-covered face upward only to find an interested spectator standing by who'd bring out the inevitable—Aren't you? etc.—Strangely enough, they never seemed to be around when one was doing well. Of course it didn't really *matter*. When learning to ski one inevitably falls down, but there are times when a decent turning away of the head is indicated.

Sometimes a keen type would swoop up to me as I stood at my take-off point watching my husband go down and ask the same question. I would say yes if he was upright and no if he was flat on his, thereby creating the impression on the slopes that my husband, like Hitler, had a double. I hope I haven't given the impression that I didn't fall down too. I did, much more often, but the point is that I was always able to pick myself up in peace, without having to make long introductions.

Later, in the lift queue, the unwelcome observer would be lying in wait, either bursting with skiing hints or wanting to discuss Schweppes affairs, neither of which were welcome topics to Teddy at that point. All he wanted was to be left alone to concentrate on what had gone wrong and, like everyone else, to enjoy himself. If Teddy happened to be ahead of us in the queue, Charles and I would sometimes overhear someone say, "Do you see that guy up ahead—He's Commander Whitehead." We would stiffen. We could never decide whether immediately to say, "Before you go on, we'd better tell you we're his family," or succumb to the temptation to listen to some home truths. When we did listen we found there were lots of inaccuracies but, in spite of extremely free discussion, never, as far as I can remember, was there any meanness. He was always the good guy, which is as well, because had they hinted otherwise he'd have been well defended by his family.

In the midst of a, shall we say, family argument when sitting in the car, when we were putting our points across to each other rather grimly, it would be disconcerting to have someone lean on the car door and say, "Aren't you Mr. Schweppes?" We'd have to stop and smile falsely and, even more maddening, we'd forget afterward what we'd been arguing about.

I was reminded again of my own role when skiing. Very occasionally we would have a ski instructor to put us through our paces for an hour. The instructor would sail gracefully away, skis firmly together, and do a beautiful skidding stop. When the three of us were there we'd make Charles go first to give us confidence; there'd be yodeling cries and "Good, Charles!" from the instructor. Next Teddy would go and there'd be encouraging noises from Charles *and* the instructor as Teddy skidded to a halt. Then I'd take off, but before I'd even gathered myself together I'd notice the instructor would be deep in conversation with Teddy and, before I had a chance to try my christie, they'd take off down the hill and I'd have a hard job finding them for the rest of the hour. It's as well that I am the dogged type or I'd never have learned to stop until I reached the car park.

There were times, of course, when Teddy was not displeased at being recognized. By attractive women, we noticed, but I won't go into that at this point. One of the more

140

pleasing examples of recognition occurred in Chicago at the Attic Club, where he was lunching with friends. Feeling a tap on the shoulder, my husband looked up and immediately recognized the man who said, "Commander Whitehead? My name is Adlai Stevenson. I'd like to meet you." As he got to his feet my husband protested, "Of all the people who need to introduce themselves by name, you, sir, are the last."

Incidentally, we have never failed to appreciate the courtesy of most Americans who, even when they have met one two or three times before, open a conversation by reminding one of their name and where we met.

Oh, the agony of being greeted in familiar terms by someone whose face one just can't place! But it happens all the time.

Crossing the Atlantic to England once, in the "Queen Elizabeth," we met dozens and dozens of people whose names I was determined to remember. When we discovered that many of these same people were to return to America six weeks later, as were we, in the same ship, I even wrote down some of the names in a little book. On the first day of the return voyage, I walked round the ship accompanied by a young Englishman who was going to the United States for the first time and was agog to meet Americans. We met lots of Americans that day, but not one name could I remember. Or face. Had I met those faces on the other crossing, or had I met them somewhere before? Or were they people who'd been on board, but whom we *hadn't* met? I just didn't know —my little book had disappeared too. Finally, after stalling like mad I saw a man sitting alone in one of the public rooms. He half smiled at me. I knew definitely that this man had been on board when I crossed to England. I swept up to him and said, "Hullo, how nice to see you again—I know we met in this ship before—I'd like you to meet Mr. ———." The little man got up and said, "We didn't actually meet, ma'am. I play the fiddle in the dance band." Well, it had been a very good band, I remember.

CHAPTER 19

WE had learned a lot more about the American Educational System by this time. We fould that private schools existed in many communities and parents sent their children to them for the same reasons that we had sent Charles to his first school in London. We learned that families moved to such places as Greenwich and Fairfield where the Country Day Schools provided the kind of education that would almost certainly ensure their being later accepted at a good Eastern prep school. These American parents, just like their English equivalents, were trying to provide their boys with the best education they could afford.

We did not see the inside of a Country Day School but we have met the product frequently and we are impressed. Generally speaking, these are the children of well-to-do Americans but although they undoubtedly have everything handed to them on a plate they are certainly not soft. To see these young boys sail a boat or ski is an eye-opener, especially when one reads about pampered American children. However, much as we admired the product of these schools we felt it was a disadvantage that the children were all of a type even before they went there. In the circumstances the school which even at that young age should have the effect of broadening a child's outlook not only in the field of education but also in the field of human relations had nothing to offer. This, of course, is the big problem of children growing up in the closed atmosphere of a rich community, not knowing how the other half lives.

Edward's affairs (business ones, I mean) were keeping him in New York for so much of the time that the decision to make our headquarters in the city was being forced upon us anyway. Family life had been very sparse and by moving we hoped at least to have some time together in the evenings.

With all these things in mind we decided to send Charles to one of the reputable boys' schools in New York City, where it transpired he did his lessons with the offspring of Americans of all religious affiliations, Europeans, Chinese, Latin Americans, a widely varied group of actors and attorneys, business men and ballplayers, socialites and sea captains, publishers and playboys, surgeons and stockbrokers, photographers and physicians, and poets and philistines.

The headmaster of the school had been born in England. Some of the masters were American, some were English. And they were all male except for a few women teachers who taught the very youngest boys. We were already beginning to feel that boys in America, especially the ones who go to coeducational schools, spend far too much time with females, so the almost entirely masculine atmosphere of the school was what we wanted for Charles.

I know my son hadn't cared very much for the idea of having lessons with girls, because when we went to his first school for a concert and the children walked in hand in hand, boy and girl, he dropped his partner's hand like a hot brick when he saw us, and refused to sing. He told me afterward he was *actually* singing but he found it wasn't necessary to move his lips. He had also become disenchanted with a small girl who had reported him to the teacher for not placing his hand on his heart when facing the Stars and Stripes and singing "God Bless America" every morning. "I shouldn't have to," said Charles aged five. "I am British." However, there were no problems of this sort at his new school, though he had to adjust in other ways. He had to learn not to get furious when the other boys ragged him when they got to the part in American History where the trained British troops were beaten by the Minute Men. In the history book that we had read to him, "Our Island Story," the British would never have suffered such an ignominious defeat. We remember our daughter being shocked in the same way when she read, at the age of twelve or so, Hendrik Van Loon's "History of Mankind," in which he says that "England is peopled by immigrants who traveled steerage from Europe, and if fate had been really kind the tide which made the English Channel would have swept over the whole of the British Isles, obliterating them, and thereby saving the world an awful lot of trouble." How mean!

Another thing Charles had to cope with was spelling. He had been very good at spelling and in his first year at his new school his teacher was an Englishman—or rather a Scot —so they spelled words the same way. But in his second year he had an American teacher, who made big red marks all over Charles's books when he wrote such words as honour, pyjama, cheque, colour, aeroplane, and centre—though we are delighted to report that the Americanization of English spelling stopped short of nite and brite.

When Charles asked what was wrong with his spelling he was told, "You're in an American school now so you must learn to spell the American way." Quite right, too. He can now write in both languages.

At this school there was far more discipline than he had met at the other school. Jackets or blazers and ties were a must, as in most English schools. We think a sloppy attitude toward dress is a reflection of the personality, and if children are allowed to go to school looking like beatniks their behavior will inevitably be less controlled. There are limits, of course, but I won't at this stage describe the tortures my son had to endure when he finally went to his English school and had to wear a tickly tweed suit and a stiff collar.

As English is the language most generally spoken in America, we were interested in its different uses. I used to wonder how children who saw printed notices which told their parents to "Drive Slow" could ever understand the proper use of an adverb. This notice used to irritate me so much I wanted to steal out in the small hours and add the "ly" to as many

144

signs as possible. I suppose Americans get the same feeling when they read signs in London, telling them to "Walk warily." Then there's "Do you have?" instead of "Have you?"

The elderly mother of a British Consul General was asked by her American dinner partner, "Do you have children?" She replied, "I used to, but no longer, I am rather old for that sort of thing."

Apart from different usages, which we all had to learn, there is fun and, if one fails to see the funny side of it, a source of endless confusion in differences in nomenclature.

To quote just one example. The English car is called by Americans, with their passion for brevity, an automobile. Similarly, a lift man (Eng.) is called an elevator operator (Amer.) A car's front end, or bonnet (Eng.) is a hood (Amer.), which I thought was a gangster (Amer.). But the hood of an English drop-head coupé is known as the top of an American convertible.

The parts of a car that suffer most frequently from collisions, which the English call wings or mudguards, are known in America as fenders, while fenders (Eng.), used to fend off the other fellow, are called bumpers in America, and I can see why. When traveling by car the English put their luggage in the boot, and the Americans put their luggage in the trunk. An Englishman caught putting his baggage in the trunk would probably be arrested, however naughty the young woman had been.

Then there are notices that I have found misleading. Seeing one which said "Flats fixed," I was disappointed to find that this was not a place where we could have our apartment redecorated. By the same token I have confused Americans by asking them to direct me to the ironmonger's which we later found to be called the hardware store.

Small-size Americans have looked at us in amazement when we tell them to walk on the pavement. "But we'll be knocked down by a car," they say, "we have to walk on the sidewalk."

While we are on the subject of words, I must mention one (though a chapter largely about schools is perhaps not the proper place for it) which just should not be uttered in polite society in England. Fanny, which is charming as a girl's name, is permissible in America when used to refer to the portion of the anatomy on which one sits. But in England, in my circles anyway, "fanny" defines part of the female anatomy which is never, but never referred to in public. If the American fanny is cold, or large, or anything, our advice is not to blazon it abroad.

As well as different words, we sometimes have problems with pronunciation or accents: ours. When we moved into our second house in Connecticut, we had a lovely time sweeping the fallen leaves and burning some of them, until we set fire to our neighbor's garden. While the rest of the family got busy with hoses I rushed to the telephone to call the Fire *Brigade*. The telephone operator was completely foxed.

Then there was the taxi driver who having been asked to drive us to the 57th St. Cinema, stopped at the 5th Ave. Synagogue, and said this was the nearest one so far as he knew.

My accent certainly stood me in good stead one day when I emerged from a shop to find a piece of paper reposing under the windscreen wiper of my car. A passerby told me it was a ticket and I'd better take it to the police station. Feeling rather nervous, never having been arrested before, I confronted the policeman on duty who told me I had parked my car facing the wrong way. "Goodness," I said, "in England we can park facing either way." "Show me your driving license," he said. "I never carry it with me in case I lose it," I said, "but I'll get it for you if you wish."

Half an hour later I was back. The policeman studied my driver's license and said, "This isn't an American license." "I know," said I, "but we have a reciprocal arrangement whereby I can use my British license until it expires whereupon I am required to qualify in America." "Gee, ma'am,"

146

he said. "I can't understand a word you're saying," and giving me a little book of driving rules he sent me home.

There is one other incident which, while it has nothing to do with words or accents, belongs absolutely to New York.

Knowing that I was busily furnishing an apartment and a house, a friend told me about auction sales. Attending which, I may say, can become an incurable disease.

The first time I decided to go to one I walked along 79th St. to the Plaza Art Galleries. I entered a quiet room and was greeted by a somber-looking fellow. "Is there an exhibition today?" I asked. "Are you a relative?" said he. "Relative?— Do I have to be? I thought this was a public auction," I said. "Madam," I was told, "the auction rooms are next door. This is a funeral home!"

There is endless discussion between people who know both countries as to whether the British are, in fact, better educated. Age for age, they are. They begin younger and they are worked harder. Moreover, the very much smaller proportion of college graduates in Britain does not mean that they have finished at a lower level. A boy or girl who passes what used to be called Matriculation—certainly Higher School certificate—in Britain is probably as far ahead as the average American college graduate.

Against this, I find it difficult to support the English argument that a boy of, say fourteen, at school in America is two years behind a British schoolboy of the same age, is necessarily a bad thing. The American boy seems to be diverted by too many extracurricular activities, but on the other hand, he gets there in the end and, in the process, has a much better time during his school years. He lacks discipline perhaps, but generally speaking he turns out to be a very nice young man, with good manners, and wide interests.

In one respect I think the American boy *is* at a disadvantage. He is not encouraged to read widely enough and he doesn't learn to express himself well, verbally or in writing.

His vocabulary is too small; he lacks skill at stringing words together.

This said, I repeat, the average graduate of the better American university is every bit as attractive to meet as his British equivalent, with considerably easier manners, especially in mixed company.

CHAPTER 20

VERY soon I found I had settled into a groove once more. It was in a different country, and the groove was perhaps wider, but I found myself doing all the things I had been doing in England before America had loomed on our horizon. I still had to dash madly away on Friday evenings. Never shall I forget the first time I drove myself along the Bruckner Boulevard. We are second to none in our admiration and praise for the great new roads in America. The Merritt Parkway is beautiful. The great Thruways with their clover-leaf flyovers are most impressive, but the various corrugated roads leading out of New York and the enormous unmarked holes that trap the unwary driver in the City itself do nothing to promote the image of efficiency.

At first I was very scared on the Bruckner Boulevard, but I learned to keep my eyes straight ahead when driving and not waver. It's less confusing for everyone. At that time I was driving a small English car, a Morris Minor, and this I found brought out the gallantry in the souls of the drivers of those enormous trucks that charge along at such speed. I was slightly worried by the possibility of being swept up in their slipstream. Invariably, no doubt having observed my expression in the driving mirror, they would wave me on.

But when we got to our house in Connecticut, the problems were not quite the same as they had been in England because, joy of joys, central heating made life so much easier. When arriving in the winter it was heaven to find the house gently warm, to touch the thermostat and have lovely hot air burst forth in every room. Still, heaven though it is, central heating can be a curse. There's this awful business of not opening windows because of the loss of heat, so that most houses have the same air inside that happened to get trapped there in the autumn when the storm windows were put up. I know there is some system whereby air is circulated but as the outlet—or is it the inlet?—is usually situated in the basement or garage it must be positively dangerous. We must confess to still preferring cool rooms with a log fire to sit by, though we admit that central heating, like Americanisms, creep up on one and when we go home to England we are not at all happy to sit in a dining room with one tiny one-bar electric fire, usually placed behind the host's chair because of his back.

I was in London in February recently when the pale sun filtered through the gray skies and my daughter came into my room and said, "How lovely to see the sun," and flung open the window. I hadn't the courage to say that I had become soft and was in fact wearing long johns under my nightgown.

There is something about the sun in England though. Everyone there worships it. It is like the sudden smile on the face of a person not given much to smiling. It is a blessing, and I will admit, when the sun does shine, it has a quality that cannot be equaled anywhere.

So we pursued our lives in much the same fashion as we had at home. This was not through any particular effort on our part to reject the American way of life. Where we now found ourselves in the country the people were very similar to the friends we had in England. Some were rich, some were not so well off, some had large houses and a staff of servants, others had a "daily" or no help at all, but they all seemed normal to us. Perhaps they drank a little more than the equivalent group in England, and there certainly had been more divorces, but this is not surprising, because divorce is not so easy to come by in England.

It is not for me to compare American and English women; this is something a man should do, but I can at least say what I admire about this particular group of women. They all seem to live busy lives, driving their children to school, dancing lessons, sailing with their husbands, playing golf, tennis, skating, skiing. Yet they never look sloppy or fussed. I have been trying very hard to think of one occasion when I have seen an American woman of this particular group look the way I sometimes feel, but to no avail. They are trim, good looking, efficient, energetic, and bright. I only hope they are sufficiently bright sometimes to blow up behind the scenes or they'd be impossible to live with.

In the time that we have been in America, my husband has often been asked how American women strike him and his reply is that so far none have. But he does sometimes criticize their uniformity of appearance, style, voice and inflections, way of laughing, and general deportment. The standard is high but it is apt to be rigidly adhered to. Against this he argues that American women, particularly the young ones, are far more forthcoming, far more aware of their social obligation to entertain as well as be entertained. They are aware of the fact that their hostess didn't ask them to dine because she thought they were hungry.

Bikinis, I believe, only arrived on the beaches in 1963—and even then they weren't really bikinis but two-piece bathing suits. Actually, we think American women showed great discrimination in not adopting the bikini, which to our mind is essentially for lying down and sunbathing. Anything more ridiculous than the lower back view of even a pretty girl walking away from one, in a bikini, is difficult to imagine. It's the beetle-bottom effect that is so unbecoming. Nudity is much more attractive. Still, Bermuda shorts have been adopted nationally, and they do nothing, but nothing, for the female form, unless it happens to be a very boyish one. The maddening thing is that Bermuda shorts are so useful. I loathed them when I first saw them. In England we had worn short shorts or long pants, and I continued to wear these when I came here. However, living in the country I found I couldn't shop in short shorts any more than I could or would

151

in England, and long pants were too hot in the unaccustomed high temperatures and humidity. So I began to see the reason for Bermuda shorts, though I resisted for three years before finally succumbing. We remember talking to Shorty Trimmingham, from whose emporium in Bermuda the popular American garment emanated. He said he was certain that Bermuda shorts would be adopted in England. This was approximately nine years ago and it hasn't happened yet. It must be the climate. If there is any sun at all people want to get their legs brown all the way up. If there isn't any sun, it's so cold one is forced into long pants. I think the final word on Bermuda shorts has been uttered by Johnny Carson, who said that the back view of the wrong sort of woman wearing them reminded him of two small boys fighting under a blanket.

To go back to American women. In London I have often been told by people that the most attractive Americans they have met have been college girls. Everyone seems to admire their looks, their manners, and their interest in the things around them. People always comment on their good grooming, being surprised no doubt to find such a passion for neatness in young ladies of somewhat intellectual turn of mind. Our own young intellectuals, on the other hand, conform to a different standard. If you see a young woman with black stockings, high-heeled shoes, long straight hair center-parted and hanging down over the face, black-rimmed eyes, and pale lipstick, she may well be about to get a First at Oxford. The debutante daughters of the aristocracy may allow themselves to be decked out in white for Queen Charlotte's Ball, but the lacy stockings, the leather coat, and the wild pony hairdo are the things that really express her inner soul.

The same with young men. They may, as my son does, have to wear sober garb for school, but in London the long-haired, leather-jacketed, tight-trousered youth is quite likely the son of one's best friend, having a week end away from Eton.

We used to hear a lot about the tedium of the English Sunday; and before I had been anywhere else I was prepared to believe that perhaps it was tedious. London, we were told, is impossible on a Sunday. No theaters, and the licensing laws are hopeless. We haven't spent many Sundays in London, so have never been affected by these things, but this we can say. To our mind any big city is loathsome on a Sunday. There is a gloom over a city when its shops and offices are closed. This applies to New York, Paris, Chicago, Geneva—anywhere—so we must defend the British Sunday. All the sensible English go for a nice long walk anyway and probably get back too tired for theaters and pubs.

For the poor visitor in London for only one day, which happens to be a Sunday, we can only advise him to talk to the hall porter of any hotel and he will be shown the ropes. Then he'll no doubt go home saying the British are an immoral lot.

This last reminds me of a man I met in an elevator in New York. We were obviously going to the same party so he introduced himself. I have a vague recollection of talking to him for ages in the elevator, but I suppose we must have got out. There were so many people that it only felt like talking to someone in a crowded elevator. He was an unusual American at a party in that he looked terribly grim. He wasn't very forthcoming, but I was stuck with him so to make conversation I asked him if he knew England. "Yes," he said. I tried again. "Were you there during the War?" "Yes." Then archly, because I was desperate, I asked "What do you think of English women?" "I think they're dreadful," he said. I was becoming unhappy with this chap. I tried to look as un-English as possible. There was no escape. We were surrounded by a shouting mass of bodies. "Why?" I screamed finally. "Because," he roared, "during the war they were too free with their favors." "And you," I shouted, "are complaining?"

We can mention here another point which proves that the British, at least the ones we know, are not stuffy. We used to sail to a place called East Head on Chichester Harbor. This was a lovely, steeply shelving beach. There were sand dunes and clumps of tall waving grasses. Plovers laid their eggs among the white pebbles. At high tide it was unapproachable from the mainland, so it was a favorite spot to sail to for picnics. There were no "amenities" and to prepare for swimming before the picnic lunch or tea we had to disappear behind a sand dune. We were always trying to invent tent-like garments under which we could disrobe. A large towel was never enough because the wind was usually pretty strong. Females therefore went behind a dune if there was one vacant or wriggled under their little tents, but the male of any age wrapped a towel round his waist and did an extremely unprovocative strip tease. There was one moment when the male, depending on which end he had decided to uncover first, looked decidedly unalluring. One might perceive the unbecoming sight of a pair of legs—possibly wearing socks which made it worse—sticking out from under a shirt. One with long tails in the English fashion, which hid the towel. On the other hand, the apparition might have divested himself of everything but the towel, and now would be struggling to get his second foot into the leg of his bathing trunks. Very difficult in a high wind. But these were everyday sights to us, and no one really noticed them. This then, was the scene that met the eyes of an American lady, newly arrived in England, who was to join some friends of ours on the beach. The tide was out, so she had been escorted from the mainland, and had to walk the whole length of East Head beach to join our party. When she arrived she was almost speechless. She was an awfully nice woman and I can see now that she didn't really want to say anything about it. But she did. She said, "These people are *British?*—but they're all undressing in broad daylight. I've just seen a man standing there in his shirt talking to a woman. It's indecent. They can't be English! In America we'd never allow that—we have little huts for people to undress in." We were all hoping she'd go away before we had to dress ourselves but she didn't, though she kept her head turned resolutely seaward while the gentlemen of our party tried to uncover as little as possible—which was, in fact, much more suggestive.

We are glad to say that at the end of the season when the American lady's son arrived and looked round for a little hut to change into his bathing trunks, she handed him a tiny towel and said, "When in Rome, my dear boy, do as Rome does."

There is a difference between the American and British attitudes toward morality and what is regarded as right and proper, though in our ten-year sojourn in America we have noticed changes, particularly in the theater, in spite of the fact that there is still a preponderance of long-run musicals. Without doubt Puritan influences have survived to this day. One is always surprised by the loneliness of beaches on a lovely Sunday morning and the police-directed traffic jam outside the churches. Everyone, but everyone, is in church. The very fact of multiple marriages is a manifestation of puritanism: legalizing the natural urge to stray which the marriage laws are supposed to frown upon. Terribly moral, but the result of these many marriages and easy divorce is, to my mind, the most immoral thing in America. Alimony! When young able-bodied childless women can demand large pensions in return for having bestowed their favors for a short period on some poor fellow, hamstringing him in any future marriage, that, I think, is the very end. And when a man, as sometimes happens among the rich, accepts a settlement, surely there is another word to describe this kind of relationship.

In making a sweeping statement about puritanism in America one exposes oneself to the risk of being asked, "What about the same sort of thing in Britain where there are also pockets of people who are puritanical and narrow-minded?" In fact, one of the difficult things about being Welsh is that the English are always telling us that we as a nation are narrow-minded as well as other unpleasant things; whereas we, the Welsh, know ourselves to be gay and poetic and great producers of leaders for the British Government and that the English make these statements to cover up their own sense of guilt in having absorbed our country.

When one remembers that the not-so-far-back ancestors of most Americans were hard-working, tough people who left their mother countries to seek their fortunes in a strange land it is not difficult to understand why, having achieved financial security, they reverted to the puritanical rules for their families. Only pretty rigid rules of conduct upon the whole community would ensure their being able to enjoy the decent life they had been striving for—after they'd had the best time amassing their wealth, of course! Which is as it was in England. The tough, the brave, the unscrupulous were rewarded with land and titles by a grateful monarch. Whereupon families were established, rules were made to safeguard their interests and so on just like America, only a longer time ago.

In American there is one hangover, presumably from those early days when rules had to be made and enforced, which to my mind is an appalling encroachment on private life. It is policemen having the right to shove torches (flashlights) into parked cars, probably without even a warning cough. How *very* embarrassing it must be.

We admit to being a little prudish in some ways. On arrival in New York and wishing to buy what are coyly referred to in England as "intimate female necessities," one wandered in and out of drug stores and chemist's shops searching in vain for one with a female assistant. When later one shopped at a supermarket one was staggered—even shocked—to find that husbands took these useful commodities off the shelves, piled them on top of the week's groceries, and pushed them unconcernedly around.

Another small shock was hearing a television commercial presumably directed at children, since it was on The Mouseketeers, which suggested that they should buy their mothers a razor for a Mother's Day present. My young son was surprised to learn that although his father did not shave, his mother did. A fact I had expected to conceal from him for several more years.

Well, America, to the British, is a foreign country.

CHAPTER 21

WE were getting used to hearing Edward labeled "celebrity" though this was not a word we would have applied to him. It was because he refused to accept the fact that some people in the United States thought of him as public property that he found himself in situations that were not exactly embarrassing but neither were they enjoyable.

The time came when we found it impossible to stand in line (queue, Eng.) for a good movie (film, Eng.), or to go to a snack bar for a quick cup of coffee without attracting attention. Neither standing in line nor visiting snack bars had ever appealed to my husband. Actually, it was a very rare occasion that would find him doing either of these things, but sometimes there was nothing else for it. It got to be awfully trying, though. We are all exhibitionists up to a point, but surely one wants to be on exhibition only when one is in the mood. Teddy himself has the capacity to avoid catching anyone's eye unless he wants to, but I always feel restive under microscopic examination by strangers. I used not to feel thus; possibly it is a sign of reduced confidence in oneself. Goodness—one cannot be on show all the time—but actually I think I was pretty game. When people came up for an autograph when we were together I would detach myself, knowing from experience that if I stayed around I would either be ignored, which would somehow offend me, or when Teddy dragged me into the conversation I would "give" far too much in an effort to appear not to resent the intrusion.

I answered quite well to my new name: Mrs. Schweppes or Mrs. Schwepees was all the same to me.

Teddy was not at all keen on losing his own identity, and while he knew that "Mr. Schweppes" on the lips of a stranger meant that the name of his product had penetrated his consciousness, it gave him no satisfaction except for the pleasure he got from thinking the chap might now buy it. This often happened. We'd be told: I saw you on Park Avenue the other day, Mr. Schweppes; I was so intrigued to find you really existed I bought some of your Tonic. Well, to demonstrate my growing Americanization, big deal! Other people protested that they drank nothing else but and we must say here and now that most people in America were extremely polite in their approach, but they did approach. The difficult ones to cope with were the slightly inebriated, especially women, who having dined well but not too wisely, had acquired the courage to approach a strange, in the unintroduced sense, male, who they supposed would not mind if they stroked his beard. Teddy has a horror of women who are under the spell of the grape or grain, and to have that combined with his other unfavorite thing, aggressiveness in the female combined with a tendency to maul, positively ruined his evening.

Many's the time we had to leave a pleasant spot where we had hoped to hear some good jazz. I didn't really care for the role of bodyguard, but it was inevitably thrust upon me. After all, a woman who had won a debate with Sir Frederic Hooper to preserve the beard was certainly not going to allow any woman in a bistro to stroke it in her presence. I sometimes wonder what would have happened if I had accosted a couple sitting harmlessly together and leeringly asked the man if I could stroke his bald head? I became known as the Gorgon's Head or the Kiss of Death, very clever at detecting possible attackers, but sometimes a female would get under my defenses and soon, as I said before, we'd find ourselves in a taxi going home. One has had time to wonder what the more persistent females hoped to gain from those encounters with a man who was "spoken for." Especially when I, who had spoken in a loud voice many years before, was present. Perhaps that is the clue. The many years. One would wish to disabuse any younger female of the idea that a long-standing wife has "had it" and is content to sit back benignly while someone else takes over the task of entertaining her husband. When the years creep up on her she will undoubtedly be agreeably surprised to find that her interest in what makes the world go round is by no means diminished and if she is really bright her husband will be well aware of it.

A difficult situation might have developed in our matrimonial world if one had not been a little bit understanding or if Edward had not cleverly managed to extricate himself from the public attention of unknown females without being so brusque that they would vow never to drink his product again and yet with sufficient aloofness and determination to satisfy the wife in me that he wasn't enjoying his situation.

Men would sometimes attach themselves too. But it was never quite so unpleasant, though often even more boring. It was more difficult to get away because we'd be held down by a hand pressing firmly on each of our shoulders.

After this little diatribe perhaps it is difficult to believe that Americans *were* usually polite. Obviously, the more sophisticated the people the less likely they were to regard my husband as part of the entertainment. Also, the method of approach made all the difference.

I had got quite used to sitting for ages while someone, man or woman, told me how wonderful they thought Teddy was. But I defy any woman, however much she loves her husband —and I am in the enthusiastic category—to take hour after hour of complimentary remarks about her spouse. One can happily absorb and encourage extravagant remarks about one's children; indeed, one keeps the conversation going oneself if there is a pause. Anything nice anyone can possibly think of to say is accepted as fact. But anyone "going on" about one's husband is different again. One begins by agreeing. Of course he is handsome, charming, kind, witty, etc., etc.—one hopes one has given the impression that only such a paragon deserves one's life devotion. But it goes on and on and on, until one begins to get an inferiority complex or one feels one should say, Oh I don't know, he's not *that* good. I have succeeded to a small extent in stopping the flow. After the first half-hour I say, Let's talk about you! How is your wife—how *lucky* you are to have her—she must be *such* a help to you in your business—she has *such* a great capacity for getting on with people—however did you *manage* before you persuaded her to marry you? When a woman joined in the hallelujah chorus I found it beneficial to say, But what about your own husband? He is obviously so attractive to women. "What do you mean?" she'd ask, the light of battle mingling with the look of disbelief in her eyes.

I was initiated into the difficulties of wifehood in polite society at a dance in New York.

A truly handsome man had been looking at me with interest across the table and I wasn't a bit surprised when he asked me to dance with him. He was a very good dancer and we swayed round the floor in rather a fetching manner, I thought. Then he spoke. "Mrs. Whitehead," he said, "I just love your husband—do tell me all about him." That taught me not to think of myself as a *femme fatale*.

The other thing is seating plans. If we invited four other people to dine with us at a restaurant, it would be my responsibility as the hostess to arrange the seating. If there happened to be a floor show, I would place the two ladies in the best positions facing the floor on the banquette, Teddy, as host, sitting between them. This would leave me, with my back to the floor, with the two gentlemen guests on my left and right. Not so when we were guests. Our hostess would say gaily, I want you to sit here, Commander. Teddy would slide onto the banquette, facing the room naturally! The hostess and the other lady would arrange themselves alongside, and I would take my usual seat with my back to the floor with waiters brushing my hairdo. The only consolation would be that I would be opposite Teddy so I could give him a wifely kick on the shins when it was time to leave, which was soon. I hear, and hear is the operative word, that there are some very good floor shows in New York.

Sometimes a man would come up to Teddy in a restaurant and say, Hi, Commander. Teddy, not knowing at that point if the man was someone he had met before, would rise to his feet. Then he'd be trapped. The man would say, "I was present when you made a speech at ——— and I want you to meet my lovely wife." Teddy would be dragged off. The lovely wife (how *kind* some husbands are) would sit there simpering and Commander Whitehead's lovely wife would be left there fuming, but wearing for the benefit of the world in general what I now think of as my Nixon smile. A smile intended to cover up the fact that deep down inside one was just a teeny-weeny bit hurt at always having to play second fiddle.

These are just a few of the difficulties of tagging along with an easily recognizable person. There are distinct advantages too, and they certainly outweighed the disadvantages or we would have gone home long ago. Even the few difficulties I have mentioned did not diminish our enthusiasm for America. We recognized them as part of the price we had to pay, and adjusted our lives in such a way that we were caught in awkward situations as infrequently as possible.

Charles was remarkably unaffected by the publicity. He just didn't seem to notice it. How any man can get a swelled head when he is a father is difficult to imagine. No father I have ever met would be allowed to show off in front of his family. My family got what they needed from a father, love, encouragement, a little discipline, and not too much interference. Charles would sometimes say he liked a certain photograph but in spite of movies and pictures in *Life* and other magazines, hundreds of newspaper articles, interviews on television and radio, Charles never commented, until one great day when Teddy appeared in *Mad Magazine*. For a while he looked at his father with new eyes. "Golly, Dad, you've made *Mad!*" He was only equally impressed when his father was commanded to present himself at Buckingham Palace for an Investiture, and we suspect part of Charles's pleasure then stemmed from a night off from school to accompany him.—Oh, there was one other thing. Some almost life-size cardboard cutouts of Teddy had been produced, which were on display in stores and supermarkets. They were extremely lifelike and when he first saw them Charles asked if he could have one. Teddy was touched. When it arrived Charles said, "Golly, Dad, what a lovely target for my bow and arrow." Needless to say, I would not allow him to treat the image of his honored parent with such disrespect.

This cardboard cutout suffered some vicissitudes. A pair of burglars engaged in robbing a safe caught sight of it in the half-light at the end of a passage, dropped their tools, and ran. Caught later, they confessed to the police their reason for bolting. This was reported in the local newspaper from upstate New York.

On another occasion a lady borrowed one of the cutouts from a shop, intending no doubt to play a practical joke with it. However, she had forgotten to tell her maid about her latest acquisition. The maid opened a closet door, screamed loudly, and rushed to call the police. When the police arrived she was able to tell them no one had left the house, so in they went with guns drawn. "Come out, we know you're there," they said to the closed closet door. No response. One policeman pulled the door open, and there was Edward's image.

Apropos of this cutout, which many people told me they had had the greatest fun with when they had put it in the ladies' changing room when giving a party: no doubt in telling me this they were seeking to beguile me, but, uproariously funny though the party may have been, one was somehow not amused, either by the idea or the telling.

CHAPTER 22

AS time went on and Charles settled down at school circumstances required that I travel a great deal with Teddy. During the early pioneering days he was moving quickly from place to place without me, but once the foundations of his business had been laid in major cities all over the United States, the work of cementing relationships involved considerable social activity. Moreover, the very nature of his business *is* social. The introduction of a top-quality mixer necessarily means a lot of mixing. In the last analysis the product that Edward was introducing is nothing more or less than a social amenity —a little better and costing a little more than domestic varieties. Since Schweppes was invariably introduced from the top down, getting to know the right people and enlisting their support in creating a demand for the product in the right places was an essential part of the job. This meant entertaining and being entertained by wives as well as husbands. We were never to repeat the hectic drive across America, though we still hope to do so one day. Instead we would stay in one city for three or four days of concentrated promotional activity. Bit by bit this grew into a series of engagements, planned in advance, following a pattern that became almost standardized. A two- or three-day visit would include a couple of major speeches at lunch or dinner, a couple of minor speeches, a dozen or more interviews with the press and on radio and television, two or three parties for drinks (at which Schweppes would provide the central theme), followed by lunch or dinner for groups of local V.I.P.'s. In time this became almost a set routine for which the pattern could be laid down in advance for those responsible for making the arrangements.

Such is the size of these United States of America and so large is its population, which could be reached only by these means, piecemeal, on a local basis, that the interviews tended to follow pretty much the same pattern everywhere. People *are* more interested in people than in things. Reporters and interviewers, acting as representatives of the people, sought to satisfy their curiosity: first, to establish that my husband actually existed as a person, as distinct from the figment of an advertising agent's imagination; and secondly, to find out whether the whole thing was originally conceived as a publicity stunt—had he grown the beard especially to attract attention to his product and exactly how did it all begin? They often expressed surprise at discovering that my husband had had his beard since 1939 and that he was in fact the President of the company in America. These revelations constituted news. The interviewers, discovering that my husband was at the beginning a more than somewhat reluctant participant in all this publicity, were vastly amused to learn of his reactions to it all, and of his experiences.

Most of these interviews were conducted in high good humor, and the fact that my husband did not "steal plugs" and showed every willingness to discuss matters other than Schweppes resulted in his being asked back on the same television programs and interviewed by the same reporters whenever he revisited any particular city. This has continued to this day.

In a very short time Teddy became bored with the subject of beards, though it continues to crop up even now. If needs be he would put up a case for beards that he didn't dream existed when he grew his nearly twenty-five years ago. Frequently he was called upon to debate "To beard, or not to beard!" But he was always delighted to find himself talking with someone willing to discuss subjects of greater interest to him. Inevitably, being fairly obviously British, he was called upon to explain differences of opinion between the British and the Americans currently in the news. It was this aspect of the job that provided Teddy with his greatest satisfaction. Having started out, postwar, explaining Britain's economic needs from the Treasury, he retained a deep and abiding interest in all things pertaining to his country and his countrymen. He was delighted to find himself penetrating parts of the country and still meeting people who had never personally met an Englishman. It was gratifying to him to have the opportunity of explaining British views on subjects about which the two countries were not seeing eye to eye. It was no less gratifying to be invited to digress upon our different attitudes and way of life.

When traveling with Teddy, as his unpaid curate, I often found myself in a similar situation. It was marvelous to have someone ask me questions and then listen to my answers. I used to say that I could not finish a sentence because English husbands always took over the conversation. But now people wanted to know what I thought about things, and I would tell them. It was lovely to *have* to talk about Britain—in spite of loving America I was and still am a tiny bit homesick.

Naturally, I was very much the understudy. I neither expected nor wanted any other role. I used to enjoy meeting all the different types of Americans in their own cities and would quite happily "hold the fort" at a party.

On one such occasion, Teddy left me at a party for two hundred people while he went to a television studio for an interview. He was accompanied by a young man who had appointed himself Teddy's guide, cum nursemaid. It was necessary in a strange city to have someone to help him get from one place to another in the shortest possible time, but this young man was, I noticed, overzealous. There was a television set in the room where the party was taking place, and at the proper time we switched it on and saw the interview. My two hundred people were very gay. I remember them particularly as a most entertaining group—but time went on, and I began to look toward the door for help. None was forthcoming. Where was Teddy? I knew the interview had ended ages ago. My group and I got our second wind and the party got going again. Time passed. No Teddy. Then in came the zealous young man. He grasped my elbow and said, "You must come with me." I immediately thought there'd been an accident. I feebly waved a general farewell and followed the young man up the stairs. Teddy was lying on his bed eating an orange. I was speechless. The young man said, "I insisted that the Commander should not return to the party. I knew that if he did, the guests would never go, and you have a dinner engagement in ten minutes." Ten minutes they gave me to repair the ravages of holding the fort alone for an hour and a half! But it was the orange that really upset me!

Teddy—loyal fellow—always said it was much easier for him when I was with him, and since I have been in America and have had the opportunity to study other businessmen away from their wives, I am prepared to believe him.

First, he knows who he is going to sit next to when in the 'plane. He can read or write or think as he wishes. When he arrives at his destination, instead of immediately rushing off to a business meeting he has to go to his hotel because his wife has to do something about her clothes. It means, instead of being entirely in the hands of whatever business associates he has come to meet, he has his own bit of home in the hotel room. We all know the dreariness of returning to a hotel room alone. However plush, the impersonalness is ultimately depressing. We have many friends—husbands—who travel alone. We know whether they're happily married or not by the way they take it. Some can, but the happily married ones get a sort of worn look at the end of two weeks. We know that they are longing to get back to their wives and families where they can be blissfully ignored. All the nicest men I know are *much* nicer when their wives are around. This brings me to another point about husbands and wives. Knowing as we do what a strain it is to spend all one's time with new acquaintances, why do so many men in America slough off old wives and begin all over again with a younger one? I know women do a lot of sloughing, too, but it is the men who have the passion for youth. To me, it seems they are depriving themselves of the very best thing in a marriage—the thing that only comes after years and years of battling it out together.

What hell it must be, having lived with one woman for twenty years and perhaps be on the edge of understanding, to begin at the bottom of the hill again. To climb laboriously back to the ledge he has just fallen off, and with someone who certainly will not understand in quite the same way that his stamina isn't what it was. And no one could convince me that the problems do not repeat themselves. Men so often marry younger versions of their old wives.

This digression possibly has no place here, except that I was reminded of it by the fact that so many husbands have to spend half their lives away from home. The expenses and income-tax situations being the way they are, wives often cannot accompany their husbands. If they don't, and there is a dinner party, another woman has to be invited to make the numbers even, so instead of the wife's dinner being charged to expenses, the dinner of some other female comes out of the profits. The other female probably drinks far more so the whole thing becomes much more expensive, apart from the risk.

There is so much more to business than sitting at a desk. So much of the real work of getting to know the people you are linking up with can only be done around the dinner table. No woman would want to be married to a man who did not enjoy having dinner with a pretty woman who is not his wife, but I am not discussing that. I am talking about the enforced kind of business party where the poor fellow gets stuck with someone he doesn't find the least bit attractive. It was ever thus.

Even our dog in England was only interested in a little bitch he had found for himself. He was a well-bred terrier and much sought after, but he wouldn't play when a match was arranged for him. Perhaps this is becoming a little basic so I'd better return to business.

Unless there is a wife around, the party given for a man can go on and on. I do think Americans have terrific stamina at business parties, though we cannot compare our situations. The business party for Teddy is often at the end of a long day of "giving out"—probably after many days of doing this. The other people are in their own surroundings. They have had time to relax a little after their day's labors. Perhaps they don't go to too many parties of this kind and are prepared to make the most of the evening. Whatever the reason they can certainly stay the course and when we are beginning to wilt they are just going into action. On the West Coast, there is also the difference in time, which *does* take a little getting used to. When I say "party" I don't mean party in the strict sense of the word. They are what would be called receptions. This means being introduced to sometimes hundreds of local people—all of whom are in some way connected with the business. It is in fact the part of Schweppes business that Teddy considers most important and the thing that he would be most loath to give up. This is public relations in its truest sense. But if after greeting perhaps five hundred people, then circulating and chatting with them, then saying good-by, Teddy has looked a little wan, I hope these friendly souls will understand. From Teddy's point of view the whole thing would be improved if the reception could take place in the open air. It's not really meeting five hundred people. It's the enclosed, usually overheated, airless atmosphere that he finds difficult to take. Fortunately, most of Teddy's business friends understand his little foibles. They know he can "give" like mad all day, but when he has to stand still for hours in a hot room, he is finished. To have a long dinner afterward is too much. I think I really proved my worth as a wife when after a long session of this sort in California I said, "Let's have dinner in bed." We did—at the Beverly Hills Hotel, and some friends came and talked to us while we luxuriated. *So,* Restoration.

Traveling with Teddy on these business trips meant that I listened to his speeches many times. Oddly enough, I was never bored. Indeed, I usually found I enjoyed the speech much more than I had at home when I sometimes had to read it or listen to it to check the timing. The atmosphere engendered by an expectant audience no doubt had something to do with my feelings. I used to be nervous in case he forgot what he was going to say—not that I had ever known him at a loss for words.

I have never been able to discover the correct procedure for a wife listening to her husband make a speech. Should one applaud in the pauses, acting as a sort of cheerleader? Or should one try to look blank? I could never look blank. The little quips Teddy introduced into his speeches to relieve the tedium would amuse me just as much the twentieth time of hearing. Our old favorite stories were always guaranteed to make me laugh. At the end of the speech I would make a gesture that was a cross between clapping and wringing my hands, which, I felt, took care of everything.

As well as listening to Teddy I also had to listen to other people making what are called major speeches. Sometimes one's attention would be held but often one would have to sit through the agony of hearing someone *read* a speech. I was glad Edward could make his speeches with only occasional glances at his notes.

Considering the fact that almost every man, certainly every businessman, cannot avoid making a speech some time and bearing in mind the frequency with which the importance of communications is stressed, it is surprising to note how indifferently most men perform on a platform. Even eminent men, whose abilities in other directions are universally acknowledged, make a poor showing when they try to communicate verbally with a large group of people. For instance, the Dutch delegate (often quoted by my husband) who, at an early meeting of U.N. observed that "The mind can absorb only as much as the seat can endure," was stating a fact that no one will contest. Yet even men who know they are not very good will drone on and on, reading stuff that appears to have been written by someone else, seemingly oblivious to the somnolent effect they are creating.

My husband has often said that no man has the right to get to his feet after dinner unless he can be entertaining. In practice he applied this rule to almost every occasion. When preparing a speech he would not seek to avoid serious subjects or even lengthy, reasoned arguments, but he would cudgel his brains, and mine, for an appropriate anecdote, quip, or sally before proceeding to the next point. By this means he hoped to keep his audience awake.

As to subject matter, he got away with murder, especially in the early days. He would talk about Schweppes, if not at the drop of a hat, certainly with very little encouragement. He was delighted to discover that the American approach to selling was substantially different from the British. He found that he didn't have to disguise the fact that the object of the exercise was to sell Schweppes and that Americans, certainly audiences of businessmen, welcomed a forthright approach.

Audiences for speeches being necessarily very much smaller than for television interviews (though there were on occasion as many as seven thousand), he could rely even more upon a constant change of listeners in different parts of the country. Having put together a not unamusing account of the early days of Schweppes—linking the beginning of the company with Benjamin Franklin, who was a friend of Dr. Priestley, who discovered how to put the fizz in water; contrasting the first one hundred fifty years of staid, somewhat tradition-bound progress of the company with its meteoric postwar development—he could usually rely upon the attention if not the positive enjoyment of his audience.

But for use on appropriate occasions he composed several

alternative speeches drawing on his pre-Schweppes experience, and, as has often happened, when he had to make several speeches to different audiences in the same city, he would be billed to speak on a different subject each time. But he fell back upon what he called the Schweppes Saga whenever he could, acknowledging that this was an out-and-out sales pitch, seeking to mitigate his sin by quoting in his introductory remarks that doyen of American literature, Mark Twain, who was wont to announce that he had sent ahead of him half a dozen alternative titles "but it doesn't matter which you chose, because you're going to get the same speech anyway."

Most of Teddy's speeches are addressed to men, service clubs predominating, conferences and conventions on a state, regional or national basis providing occasionally much larger audiences. Since his is a business approach he avoided the usual lecture circuit, but now and again he agreed to speak to a woman's club if he was going to be in the city for other purposes.

On one such occasion when he was addressing the annual dinner of a well-known ladies' club he was given the opportunity to open with a great deal of laughter by quoting directly from the letter he had received from the secretary of the club, who had ingenuously asked him to tell them about his "operation, development, and achievements."

A direct result of having introduced some humor into his speeches was that Teddy acquired something of a reputation as a raconteur. His hardiest perennial is about the Admiral and a Bishop. It concerns two small English boys who went away to school at the tender age of eight. Egged on by their fellows, and for no good reason, they fought bitterly. They bruised and battered each other severely. Thereafter, they became enemies and ceased to speak to each other. As ill luck would have it, they continued not only to the same school but to the same college of the same university. So, from the age of eight until they reached maturity, they remained in close proximity to one another; always within sight of each other, but never recognizing each other's existence. Here the story would have ended but for an incident, many years later, during the last War. One, who had become a Bishop, dressed in well-filled frock coat and gaiters, recognized the other, dressed as an Admiral of the Fleet, no less, on a wayside station in Derbyshire.

The Bishop wrestled with his conscience for fully five minutes, fighting back the devilish temptation, at this stage, to get his own back. Finally the devil won. The Bishop waltzed down the platform, drew himself up in front of the Admiral and addressed him thus, "Forgive me, Stationmaster, but can you tell me at what time the next train leaves for Derby?"

The Admiral, fixing the Bishop with an eye, but without a glint of recognition, replied, "I haven't the least idea. But in your condition, Madam, I wouldn't dream of traveling."

CHAPTER 23

ONE decision Teddy had to make when he found himself so frequently cast in the role of business party-giver and receiver concerned his own consumption of liquor. He had never been a drinking man. I don't know what he did when he was young. Most Englishmen drink gallons of beer in their early adulthood, but somehow I cannot imagine Teddy quaffing tankard after tankard of ale and being "one of the boys." Undoubtedly he did what most young people do and got himself miserably tight once or twice and thereafter vowed to be more abstemious. Not that I have never seen him soaring. One of my earliest recollections of our life together is of floating along a dark lane in Devonshire, singing loudly and trying to avoid barging into the high hedges on each side of the road. We had spent several hours in a little pub drinking rough cider, extremely potent stuff in Devonshire, and Teddy had rounded off the evening by standing up and singing *all* the verses of "Frankie and Johnny" that he could remember, plus a few he had invented.

The applause that had burst forth when he sat down possibly added to his feeling of intoxication.

A less pleasant early memory is of being invited to a champagne party and the headache that quickly followed. A rather sneaky habit was to serve very good champagne at first to get every one merry and talkative and, when the party was underway, to serve an inferior inexpensive brand. One could always tell anyway because the inferior brand would have a napkin wrapped round it to hide the label or the label would have fallen off—in the bath, where it had been cooling on ice. So one would be told if one inquired. The good champagne label would be ostentatiously displayed and appreciative comments would be encouraged. We never had the nerve to practice this deception. We just knew we wouldn't get away with it even if we had wanted to. Someone would surely have gone to inspect the bath, or we would have looked guilty, if we'd been asked what vintage.

Neither would we drink nor serve champagne cocktails. In our view this was merely a means of ruining two good drinks if they *were* good, and to us a champagne cocktail composed of an inferior wine and cheap brandy is lethal.

So Teddy was pretty abstemious and conservative in his drinking and I followed suit. As he got older he became interested in wines and developed a palate. I have never been able to compete with Teddy's winesmanship, though many's the meal we had discussing the merits of different wines. For me, white wine had to be dry and cold, and red wine had to be full-bodied (I absorbed enough knowledge to know what that meant), and served at room temperature, or warmer if in England.—Oh—and it had to breathe—and not be shaken up. Teddy was sufficiently interested to try two or three different wines at dinner, but I still labor under what I am told is a delusion that I cannot mix wines and remain happy.

An acquaintance of ours was Vice-Chairman of the Wine and Food Society of England. He was quite an old man. He resembled an English version of the man on the cover of *Esquire*. When I told him once that I couldn't take two or three different wines at dinner, he said "Nonsense" (this is one of the more maddening things Englishmen say to women). "You must have been having the wrong wines with the wrong food. I shall arrange a dinner. I shall order all the food and all the wines. I guarantee that you will feel so well afterward that you will join me for breakfast at 8 A.M., *and* you will eat porridge and bacon and eggs." The dinner was arranged at the Hinds Head at Bray, and we were all to spend the night at this delightful Inn. To quote Jorrocks, which Teddy did at the time, "Where I dines, I sleeps."

Before dinner we had a vintage champagne. (Never, never, cocktails, I was told—not that we ever, ever did.) We were allowed only one glass, which had to be sipped slowly. There was a bright log fire burning in the room where we were sitting and the heat from that combined with the champagne was already making me feel drowsy.

Dinner was an intentionally prolonged affair. Apparently one of the tricks is to let one course and one wine have time to settle before attacking the next. I am assured it was a marvelous dinner and that the wines were superb. We proceeded, I am told, through a series of fine Bordeaux (the Colonel was a Claret man)—the wines getting older as the dinner progressed. The other members of the party still talk about it, as does Teddy. For me, the evening ceased to be a pleasure after the second wine. Our kind adviser was completely unaware of this, I am proud to say. I stayed the course gamely until 11 o'clock when we all went our separate ways to bed. The last words I heard were "Don't forget—breakfast at eight."

I lay in bed feeling terrible. Teddy could not understand it. The dinner had been exceptional. *I* couldn't bear to think about it. The night dragged on and finally I slept, only to be awakened immediately by Teddy. "Time to get up if you're going to keep your appointment." I staggered out of bed and did what I could to make myself look presentable. I thought I looked ghastly. I walked carefully down the stairs as the clock struck eight. Colonel Campbell was waiting for me. "Good morning," he said. "Now wasn't I right—you look absolutely wonderful." My only relief was in thinking that wine is never, but never, served with porridge and bacon and eggs. The extraordinary thing is that I really *did* feel wonderful after breakfast.

By the time Teddy came to America he knew exactly what he liked, and how much he could drink. Perhaps a glass of sherry or Dubonnet before dinner, a glass or two of wine

176

with his dinner; maybe whisky much later if it was a long evening.

I liked gin and Tonic. Sherry invariably caused a pain in my left shoulder.

When we got to America the first thing I had to overcome was the fact that gin in the United States is of higher proof than in England and the shots are very much larger. I didn't realize it for some time. I thought New York was going to my head. I have disclosed in an earlier chapter how I coped. I had to stop going to parties. When ultimately I began doing business parties I knew enough about the power of the drinks to have only one proper one, and then to have plain Tonic, which looks the same.

Teddy, who had to do very many more of these parties than I, decided almost at once that he would not drink hard liquor at all. If he had accepted the number of drinks regularly pressed upon him it is doubtful whether he would have survived one year, let alone twelve.

Having made the decision, he was stuck and consequently he had to get through many evenings with no alcoholic sustenance.

The long sessions of drinking before dinner were overcome more or less successfully by him on plain Tonic. In some company he felt positively exhilarated without the help of liquor.

In the early days he was buoyed up during his drinkless cocktail sessions by the thought that he would have some wine with his dinner, but usually nothing would be served but iced water. This seemed to us very strange, and hardly conducive to the enjoyment of dinner. We were staggered by the number of Martinis or Scotches-on-the-rocks that could be downed before a meal.

I used to be rather nervous about mixing Martinis. We arrived in America when Martinimanship was at its peak. We had read about the business of passing the Vermouth bottle over the gin quickly in case it diluted the gin, and I had been as amused as everyone else, but nevertheless, I was nervous if I had to mix Martinis for Americans. I was forced to do so one evening. I carefully measured one part vermouth to three parts gin, and did all the other necessary things. When the first batch disappeared, rather quickly but with no apparent enjoyment, I made some more, reducing the proportion of Vermouth. These were received with a slight brightening of the eye, and when they had gone I made more again. The receptacle in which I had done my mixing was now empty. I put in some ice cubes, then poured in neat gin, adding no Vermouth. I stirred it for a short while, and poured it into the glasses. The few ice cubes had not even begun to melt so what I was serving was unadulterated gin.

My guests, on tasting their drinks, said these were the best Martinis they had ever had. Which proves that all the stories about not standing the Vermouth bottle too near the gin are true.

When Teddy was host at a restaurant he would order wine and ultimately the message got through that he did like alcohol, but not in large quantities before dinner. It was often amusing the following day to be told by a guest who had had perhaps half a glass of wine with his dinner, that he felt awfully grim, and that he attributed it entirely to the wine. Never, never, to the colossal number of Martinis or whiskies, or even gins and Tonic, he had drunk before and after.

We have noticed a great change in the American attitude to wine in twelve years. It is probably because more and more Americans are going to Europe and learning to know the wines of the countries they visit.

Obviously there have always been people here, and we have met many of them, who have a great appreciation of wines and who drink in a most civilized fashion. For instance, we remember, with great pleasure, a luncheon at the Almaden Vineyards at the delightful French Provincial house belonging to Mr. and Mrs. Louis Benoist when we were driving from San Francisco to Los Angeles. We enjoyed a repast that Colonel Campbell of the Wine and Food Society himself would have approved. The setting would have done credit to Cecil Beaton. A shaded terrace overlooking the vineyards, which spread over the gentle slopes of the hills facing the house.

The wines were selected by a true expert and we were feeling decidedly mellow as we drove on to Monterey for the night.

Next morning we had to negotiate the coast road from Monterey to St. Louis Obispo, which is just as spectacular as the Amalfi Drive in Italy. It seemed to me that our American car was far too big for the road, our front corners were suspended in space most of the time. But what a fabulous drive, with grass-covered hills of enormous proportions on one side, and huge outcrops of rock. The winding road hugging the side of the hill; great cliffs and rocks below us with the Pacific Ocean dashing and churning around them. Unlike the Amalfi Drive, in Italy where there are hundreds of pink and white houses clinging to the sides of the hill and, at least when we were driving along it, an incessant stream of horn-blowing cars charging at us so that we approached every curve with our eyes closed, the Big Sur road was completely unspoiled. No houses were visible. Nothing but the wind blowing the long grasses, the sun and the sea. We noticed an extra foaming of waves in the water out to sea. We stopped the car to try to decide what caused it. It could have been submerged rocks with waves breaking on them, but we eventually found the extra sparkle and white water was caused by the spouting of a school of gray whales migrating from the Arctic to their breeding grounds off the coast of Mexico.

A long way from Winemanship one might think, but we have another animal story which concerns wine.

Our Christmases in America are spent in the country. It has always been possible to toboggan and skate on Christmas Day, so our habit is to do these things all day and to have our Christmas dinner in the evening. Teddy had put some bottles of white wine in the snow on the steps outside the kitchen door to cool. There was also one half-finished bottle left from the previous evening, which had its cork resting lightly in the neck. We were preparing to sit down to dinner when we heard a commotion in the kitchen. Charles went out to investigate. He called us urgently. We all rushed out and tried to look out of the door. There was a 'possum lying on its back on the bottom step with the opened wine bottle resting on the next step above. Its little hands were clasped round the neck of the bottle and, with a blissful expression on its face, it was celebrating Christmas. It didn't move until it finished the bottle and neither did we. An English girl who was staying with us said, "What a marvelous country! In one day I have had my very first snowy Christmas, I have skated and tobogganed—and I have seen an inebriated opossum."

Opossums—sober or bibulous—are unknown in England.

There is one more incident to recount which proves that there are more connoisseurs of wine around than we were first aware of.

The stock of wines in our house in the country had been replenished before Christmas. We had then gone away, leaving the house unoccupied for two weeks. The first evening we dined there on our return, Teddy went to the cupboard where we kept our reserves to get a bottle of wine. After a while he called me and said, "Why have you had the wine moved?" Moving things to different places used to be a habit of mine which he deplored but now I hurriedly disclaimed all responsibility for interfering in the department which I regarded entirely as my husband's. The house was searched. The wine Teddy was looking for had disappeared. Finally we realized that all the imported wines, including champagne and sherry, plus brandy and Scotch, were also missing. But we *were* left with Bourbon and some California wines. Interesting discrimination on the part of a burglar.

The police were a little skeptical when they arrived. We had a feeling they thought we had had a bacchanalian orgy, drunk everything ourselves, and thereby achieved loss of memory. But proof arrived. Charles, who with a boy friend had been following some large tracks in the garden, came in bearing two empty bottles of Dom Pérignon '49, and a full bottle of Tio Pepé, which he had found in the snow. The tracks were familiar ones to us. They were made by Teddy's Wellington boots, which the burglar had donned to walk through the snow without getting his feet wet. *They* were imported also. The other thing that was missing was a hunting horn. Why a hunting horn? It can be imagined with what interest we eyed our fox-hunting friends thereafter. Everyone with large feet and a taste for imported wines and Scotch was under suspicion. Actually, except for the feet, I think that included everyone.

After this we decided we would not keep a large cellar, so any light-fingered gentleman with the same taste in wines as Teddy will just have to somehow get invited to dinner.

I don't know if Americans have the same feeling of possessiveness about their drinks as the English. I *do* know that when a young man caller at our house one day calmly helped himself to a large drink without being invited, Teddy eyed him very coldly, and refused afterward to do whatever it was the young man had been trying to persuade him to do. We heard afterward that this is quite common. If the drinks are on view, it is considered an open invitation. I positively shudder to think what the effect would be if a young man (or an old one for that matter) helped himself to the whisky of some irate old boys I know in England. To be given a drink in a home is an expression of hospitality, and hospitality has to be offered, not taken for granted.

After this episode we concealed our drinks until the sun had disappeared below the yardarm, when we'd be in drink-offering mood.

Perhaps the fact that some people do help themselves to drinks is the reason why so many American houses have a bar in the cellar? We used to think it was a hangover from Prohibition days, when people, possibly not caring to be surprised drinking moonshine, had gone to ground in the way that gamblers used to incarcerate themselves in secret rooms in England. We, however, couldn't help feeling that our hosts thought we were not to be trusted in the drawing room with a drink in our hands; we might get boisterous and begin beating up the furniture. Actually, there *are* rather a lot of *House and Garden* living rooms in American houses that look completely unlived in. Beautifully decorated display rooms, but life only goes on in the den or—heavens—the rumpus room.

Our final wine incident happened at a much publicized charity ball in New York.

The tickets were terribly expensive, but we were assured that this was *the* event of the season. We were also assured on the invitation that "Great Wines will be served." This statement caused Teddy's eyes to light up, so on the appointed evening we found ourselves sitting at a table with several other people, waiting for something to happen. Once again we were squashed together and waiters jostled each other, and squeezed past our chairs carrying large loaded trays at dangerous angles over our heads.

There was no menu on our table, and as it was impossible to interrupt the chain-gang activities of the waiters, we accepted the first two courses and played a sort of guessing game. The great wines failed to appear for some time but eventually a frenzied waiter began splashing wine into glasses all around the table. When he reached us Teddy said, "Just a moment—" He didn't actually say "my good man," but it sounded like that. "What wine is this?" "Red," said the waiter, and splashed on.

CHAPTER 24

THERE had been many trips back to England during the several years we had been living in America.

In the early days we had all the excited feelings of immigrants cut off from their Motherland when packing our bags for the voyage home. We could hardly contain ourselves while crossing the Atlantic. As well as being thrilled by the prospect of seeing our families and revisiting our old familiar haunts, we looked forward to the pleasure of being unrecognized in the public sense. We were a closely knit family content just to be together, but in America it was sometimes easier to do things without Edward and the inevitable audience. Sad, but true.

The newspaper man meeting the boat would interview Edward and write a piece about British Exports. This was the way Edward wanted it although an occasional British interviewer *au fait* with events across the Atlantic would want to publish a more colorful article about his business operation.

The rumblings of the "not quite the thing" group in England were already beginning to subside and changing to faint murmurs of admiration as the business in America prospered, but Edward, as British as the next man, was not going to allow any overflow of "beard" publicity to filter into his native heath. Anyway, a beard of itself is not particularly remarkable in Britain.

As time went on we found ourselves in the position of having to defend America. Often any praise of America by us was taken as criticism of Britain. If the United States made a move unpopular in Britain we'd asked, "What are *your* friends up to now?"

An acquaintance who owned a lot of land was very cross

one day to find a young man wearing the uniform of an American G.I. walking through his woods. When ordered to take himself off the soldier stood his ground, saying that the trespass laws of England allowed him to walk through the woods so long as he caused no damage. This maddened our erstwhile chum, who made threatening motions with his stick, whereupon the G.I., expert in judo as well as the law, threw him over his head.

When we met the landowner his arm was in a sling. "What happened to you?" said Edward.

"One of *your* friends did this," we were told and have been cut dead ever since.

We also have to contend with the false impression among many of our British friends that because we lived and worked in America we were loaded.

For my first two years in America I religiously kept accounts of everything I spent and found that at that stage the cost of living was three times as high in America as in Britain. By the way, this, I think, was the reason for the unpopularity of Americans in Britain and in Europe in the postwar years. It was not only the tourist who had lots of dollars to flash around, but low-ranking officials of the United States Government could live at a much higher standard than they had been used to in their own country. Dinner at the Savoy, a flat in Eaton Square, and a maid was hardly the equivalent of a house in Levittown, and evening at the pizza parlor and a baby sitter. This is a slight exaggeration, of course, but there was a definite feeling of resentment among the natives about this aspect of the transition from one country to another and the lower cost of living. Though we, the Whiteheads, in the light of our later experience think that any family uprooting itself from its own country deserves to be rewarded. It would be nice if I could say I was the kind of dedicated home economist who continued to keep accounts, but after my two-year period my interest died. However, I do know that it has become much more expensive to live in

Britain, partly because of the availability of things such as refrigerators and washing machines that used to be considered luxuries.

As for getting rich in America, what actually happened was that we were still poor but on a higher level.

Back in the United States, Edward, having defended America to the British, was busily doing a weekly program called "This Is Britain" on WQXR, the *New York Times* Good Music Station. This extracurricular activity, nothing to do with Schweppes, gave Edward a tremendous feeling of satisfaction. Having written an essay on any subject of his choosing that had something to do with Britain, he then had to dream up appropriate musical interpolations using British composers and/or performers. With the vast resources of the WQXR record library and enthusiastic assistance from his producer, he found the chore of putting his program together a welcome antidote to his daily round of business.

As I have said before, it is satisfying for an expatriate to talk about his own country and Teddy, with his love and knowledge of the countryside as well as his interest in his country's postwar development, was getting a great charge out of trying to put Britain across to his listeners.

For three years, the duration of the program, I had the feeling I had lived it all before. The format was the same as that of our Treasury days. It was Central Park instead of Hyde Park. Park Avenue instead of Whitehall. A New York apartment instead of a London house. In the country, we had squirrels in the roof in Connecticut, instead of rooks in the chimney in Hampshire. It wasn't so very different so long as we stayed inside and avoided the public gaze. Edward would disappear over the horizon on Schweppes business, then the evenings would be spent writing speeches or taping several "This Is Britain" programs to be used when he was off on his travels. Sometime I must try and work out how much time has actually been spent in the bosom of the family. It won't be very much, but what there is is good.

As a result of his radio program the recognition signals came thicker and faster in and around New York. Edward, not unnaturally, was pleased when anyone accosted him to say that they had enjoyed a speech he had made, or an article he had written, but he always looked a trifle beady-eyed when he was asked, "Aren't you the guy in the ads?" or even "Don't you play the part of Commander Whitehead?" But anyone telling him they regularly listened to his broadcasts and that they enjoyed them caused him positively to glow. A whole new group of people now accosted us on private occasions, but we did not want to brush them off. They were usually highly intelligent discriminating people. Of course. They appreciated the program. The added numbers of encroachers had one effect on Edward and one that proved to be rather expensive. All our private conversations, which we had no time for when we were together, had to take place on the telephone. Fascinating things like Had one of us remembered to pay the taxes and Would one of us see that those buttons were sewn on by Friday, were discussed long distance at up to a dollar a minute.

Ever the kind husband trying to make me feel wanted, he insisted that I go on his radio program with him on a day when he was doing a program about Wales. He wanted me to pronounce,

Llanfairpwllgwyngyllgogerychwyndrobwllllandysyliogogogoch

for him. I was fortunately able to do it. It sounds exactly the way it looks.

We continued our conversation, and as it was St. David's Day I mentioned the daffodils and the leeks and the fact that leek soup is one of the most delicious dishes to come out of Wales. It is a good nourishing country soup. A refined, sophisticated version of it called *Vichysoisse* is offered at most restaurants in New York. But the two shouldn't be mentioned in the same breath.

I received *my* first fan letter asking for the recipe. As everyone who has this soup at our house enjoys it like mad, I'll pass it on.

WELSH LEEK SOUP
1 large bunch leeks
1 bunch carrots
Parsley
Potatoes
Grated cheese

Trim the leeks, keeping as much of the green part as possible. Split them down the middle and wash carefully. Cut them into pieces about ½ inch long.

Melt a piece of butter in a large saucepan, and lightly fry the chopped leeks. Do not brown. Stir them round with a spoon.

Scrub the carrots and cut into thin slices. Add them to the leeks and stir them round for a while also.

Add enough cold water to submerge the vegetables. Bring to the boil. In the meantime peel some potatoes—about 5 or 6 smallish ones to a bunch of leeks, cut them into pieces and drop in the saucepan. See that there is enough water to cover the potatoes too. Simmer until the potatoes are soft, then add some roughly chopped parsley, and cook a few minutes longer. Add salt.

We squash it all up with a potato masher and serve it in large bowls with grated cheese and whole wheat Italian bread. Delicious.

This soup with apple pie or maybe fresh fruit and cheese afterwards is our usual Saturday lunch in the country.

On another occasion I received my second fan letter. We had been telephoned by a newspaper in Connecticut. Would we agree to have some photographs taken of the interior and exterior of our house for publication in a weekly. They were doing a series on the homes of local celebrities. How could one refuse? One didn't. But much pushing of furniture ensued and much standing in corners trying to decide which were the best features of the house. We needn't have bothered; the photographer had his own ideas, and the pictures eventually appeared in print. The published ones included one of me, looking frightfully *Tatler* I thought, sitting on a chair in a corner of the living room, elegantly toying with a guitar, on which instrument after two years of concentration I could pluck out "Greensleeves" if there was no one within earshot.

My fan letter read: "Dear Mrs. Whitehead, I noticed the Spanish Classical Guitar in the pictures of your home. Is it for sale? Yours," etc.

At different times I have been asked if I am someone else. The first time in this country was on that far-off winter's day on Long Island when I found myself beagling. Hounds were on the scent and they had disappeared through a hedge. When we, the field, reached the hedge we had two choices: we could leap gaily over it or go through a hole very close to the ground.

I went through the hole behind two tweed-skirted ladies. My face was level with their Newmarket boots when they addressed me. "Do forgive us," they said, "but are you Greer Garson?" Now, I ask you, would Greer Garson be beagling on a Sunday afternoon? And if she were, would she be allowed to wriggle through a hole in a hedge unaided?

At other times I have heard that I am the girl (girl, mind you) on the White Rock bottle. The only thing we had in common was the hairdo I affected at that time. Then there was Debbie Reynolds—at that time young enough to be my daughter. And Myrna Loy; I *liked* that. Are you Zsa-Zsa Gabor? I was asked one day. On that occasion we had had to stay in New York overnight unexpectedly, and on the following day at noon I got into a taxi wearing a short evening dress. There was something about wearing evening dress during the day that made me feel I had just come from an assignation. That, I suppose, is what the taxi driver thought, too. Any way, he was rather cross with me for not being Zsa-Zsa Gabor.

Simone-Simon? someone else asked. Then Gracie Fields. Gracie Fields had been playing the part of "Mrs. 'Arris goes to Paris" the previous night on Television and my taxi driver thought I was exactly like her in that part. Now, Gracie Fields is a darned nice woman, but in the part of Mrs. 'Arris, she had to look definitely frowsy. With all respect to Gracie Fields, *she* could have been my mother. *I* was rather cross that time.

At a theater when Edward was signing someone's program and I was trying to look aloof, a youth studied me for a while and then said, "Are you anybody?" Well honestly. I was beginning to wonder.

I don't know which of my many faces the advertising agency had in mind when they asked Teddy if I would appear with him in an advertisement for Schweppes. I had been in a mushing picture, but it was snowing at the time it was taken so my face was a pleasant blur. My foot had appeared in another sailing picture. But now they wanted a mature woman. And whyever not? They didn't have to look far. I was right there, getting maturer by the week.

One of the pictures was of Teddy and me hanging onto each other clutching our Schweppes bottles and laughing gaily. This caused another fan (?) letter to be written. Was I intoxicated? The most successful picture of all was of Teddy reclining on a bench with me pulling off his riding boot in the traditional English fashion. But to me it looked as though I was being kicked out of the picture. Most apt and significant!

My participation in the advertising did very little to alter the course of my life. I participated, I bloomed for a day, then I was quietly filed away. If I had had (which I hadn't) any thoughts of competing with my husband I was due for disillusionment. One woman in Bloomingdale's asked me if I was me, but as she was looking at my charge plate at the time, perhaps she was only checking to find out if I was its rightful owner. No—on second thoughts she did say she was an ardent drinker of Schweppes Tonic. I remember I wasn't feeling my usual dazzling self that day and her question made me realize that there are definite disadvantages to being recognized. It's no comfort to suspect that someone one has met casually is saying, "Guess who I met today—Mrs. White-head—you know, Commander Whitehead's wife. She's nothing to write home about." Whereas one doesn't mind a bit if this criticism is applied to a person one vaguely resembles and for whom one is mistaken.

Before I had appeared in the photographs, new people I met on a business trip would sometimes admit that I was not a bit of what they had expected. On probing further, I would find that as Teddy was, they understood, a typical Englishman, it stood to reason that his wife of many years' standing would also be what they imagined a typical English-woman (British woman!) to be. Reserved, refined, let's face it, dull. Tweedy, woolen-stockinged (in June, in the Middle West?), sensibly shod. Proper, well educated, a stickler for conventional behavior and a chum of the Royal Family! That's more or less what they thought was typical. How are these preconceived ideas arrived at? It *must* be old movies!

There are women in England who would fit this descrip-tion but from what I know of Teddy he wouldn't have mar-ried one or even been happy if his wife had later developed that way, which sometimes happens. Much as he thinks he likes peace and quiet.

After my appearance in the photographs I had to overcome a slight fear that people might think I thought myself a glamor girl, which thought had not entered my head for about fifteen years—or perhaps ten.

Teddy had also been irked by this thought when he had first been photographed, though it wasn't so bad for him. In America many kinds of men are considered glamorous. Big fat ones, weedy ones, all kinds, so long as they have that little extra something. But glamor in women usually means youth as well as that extra something in large quantities in all the right anatomical places. I was in no mood to enter the stakes.

So I was glad to sink back into my groove where I could be what I fondly thought of as the power behind the throne. (To my mind the best role for women at this time.) My short sojourn into the realm of the public husband-and-wife team business left me with the knowledge that it would be sheer hell to be on show, or on tap, or on call, or in any way available to the general public all the time. We wives are lucky to be asked to go along as useful adjuncts. I think women are clever, but if we're truly clever, we'll let our husbands think they are cleverer. I hope this statement will not be construed as a crack against my own husband. He, of course, *is* cleverer.

It must not be thought that when, after my brief fling, I found myself back in the groove I accepted my role without reservations. I was still uncertain as to how to behave when some ingenuous person would say to me in my husband's presence, "Don't you think you are lucky to be married to this guy?" It was one thing for me to think it, but I was darned if I was going to let anyone else say so. I was still subjected occasionally to the blind eye at various functions, but time has softened the blow. Anyway, this sort of thing happened only at what I call impersonal parties. And even then it was possible to find someone whose plight would be worse than one's own. I would find myself drawn to a man wearing a slightly defiant smile. Terribly game, you know. He was always the husband of a well-known woman. She'd be engrossed in conversation with a group who'd be hanging onto her words. Admirers. In his own field the husband might be a wizard, but his function here would be to get his celebrated wife out on time. It was a comfort to me to meet these other sufferers. We were never disloyal to our own particular spouses without whom we'd never have been asked, but we were awfully glad we had each other to talk to. At times we, the lesser-halves, would be enjoying ourselves so much that our carefree laughter would draw slightly resentful looks from our celebrities because they, for some reason, might be finding the party rather hard going.

CHAPTER 25

ENGLISHMEN—Britishers—fall in love with their motor cars. This is a fact that will be confirmed by many a long-suffering English wife whose husband has refused to have the picnic hamper on the back seat in case it scratches the upholstery. Every nick or scratch inflames them, and the fact that they often cause the bumps and scratches themselves does nothing to lessen their fury.

I *like* the American attitude toward cars. When I found they were not regarded as more precious than wives I was surprised. I cannot say I was delighted when I made this discovery, because my lord and master still retained the British attitude, and I realized almost at once that the contrast was going to cause some trouble. Used as I was to seeing cars treated gently, I was genuinely hurt at first when I saw someone pull out of a parking space by bumping backward and forward into the cars standing fore and aft. I remember taking an hour and a half to get a car out of a corner in a mews off Hill Street in London. If I had bumped backward and forward the fenders (bumpers—American) would have received a blow or two, but I'd have been out in five minutes. After a very short time in America I began to realize what bumpers are for.

The reason one was given when one asked why it was necessary to be so careful was that the car would keep its value if it were in good condition. If one sold it one would get a better price. This was unconvincing because the other thing that Englishmen don't like to do is sell their cars. They like to buy as good a one as they can afford, and nurture it tenderly for the rest of their lives.

If it develops a cough it must have a rug put over its bonnet (hood) on cold nights. It must be dried off after the rain with a very special large chamois leather. This possibly while the wife is unloading the car if she's been allowed to put anything in it. People shouldn't eat anything crumbly inside the car, the carpet would be ruined. Nothing too heavy must be put in the boot (trunk) in case the springs complain. All this tender concern for a vehicle which, they boast, is built to last a lifetime! I am sure the reason most people use seat belts in cars in England, apart from the safety factor, is that husbands and fathers have at last discovered a legitimate way of tying their families down so that their cars are not molested in any way.

I know it is possible to feel sentimental about a car. We, as a family, became very attached to an ancient Rolls Royce that Teddy acquired in the immediate postwar years. It wasn't a practical car. It had been built in 1930 for a long-legged man. Fortunately it fitted Teddy, but as the seat was fixed it was not possible for anyone with shorter legs to drive it. Three people could sit comfortably in the front seat and there was a dickey (rumble seat) which would take two more if they could stand the weather. When the car became ours it received all the care it deserved. Driving to the cottage at week ends with the hood (top) down, Teddy, Jacq, and I would feel so secure. It was built like a tank. There were no drafts because of its high sides, and best of all, we could see over the tops of all the hedges.

When Charles was born we had problems. There was nowhere in the car to put the baby. But Jacq volunteered to ride in the dickey seat so long as she could have an umbrella when it rained. She'd rather do this than sell the car. It will be observed that she liked to preserve the old familiar things, be they beards or cars.

So Charles grew up in the "Duchess," as we named our ancient chariot. Teddy would be driving, Jacq would be in the dickey giggling with a girl friend, and Charles gradually grew tall enough to peer through the windscreen with me holding on to him.

Being transported in this way, with all my family together, is one of the nicest things I remember. Riding in the Duchess meant that Teddy was home so we were all particularly happy.

Alas, though, when the decision was made for us to come to America he felt the time had come to find the Duchess a good home. He feared she would not survive the transplantation.

A neighbor in London had often cast covetous eyes in the direction of our car. He was a bachelor, and Teddy thought he might make a suitable consort for his treasure. A deal was made. I seem to remember our neighbor promising to look after the car in the manner to which it had been accustomed. Indeed, he went much further. He took the Rolls Royce chauffeur's course so that he could nurse it properly. On return visits to London we would see the car outside our neighbor's house, and sometimes Teddy would be invited to take Charles for a drive in it.

Much later, when Charles was thirteen, he was sent to school in England; Repton, in Derbyshire. During his first term, whilst still feeling a little homesick, he was looking out of his study window on a gray November day, when he saw what could only be the Duchess being driven into the yard outside. Soon there was a message: Whitehead was wanted in the headmaster's study. Charles there met a gentleman whom he vaguely recognized and was told the story.

Our neighbor was an Old Reptonian, though we hadn't known that, and he didn't know that Charles was at his old School. The car had served him well and faithfully so instead of selling it he would present it to the School for the boys to study it and admire its excellent workmanship.

There was a New Yorker in the headmaster's study. Our neighbor had said "By the way, I bought this car from Commander Whitehead whose picture you may have seen in the

New Yorker." "Just a moment," said the headmaster. He rang his bell and sent for Charles.

We now visit Charles *and* the car at school. We like to think of them there together.

A compromise has been reached in our family in the years we have been in America. Teddy has an English car he can worry about and I have an American shooting brake (station wagon) which he sometimes tries to protect, but with not much success. The American one is used for skiing and shopping and carrying things about. All one has to do is guide it. It is not, alas, entirely dependable in cold weather, and when left outside in Vermont on a skiing trip, it has to be pushed many miles at considerable speed by a jeep to get it started. Something to do with automatic change, I understand. However, although Teddy's car is modestly considered the best make of car in the world, and should presumably be utterly reliable in this kind of emergency, he refuses to use it for such mundane tasks. Anyway, if it *should* fail to start in the morning, the ignominy of being pushed would be too much for him to expect the car to endure.

I am allowed to drive this car having proved over the years that my early training has become ingrained.

On one occasion I had to take it skiing because at the last moment some small illness had put the station wagon out of commission. Charles and I were in New York City, Teddy was in Canada, and we were going to meet in Vermont for a skiing week end. Owing to the problems with the other car we left New York later than we had intended. We purred along valiantly through darkness and the beginnings of a snowstorm. Halfway to our objective I telephoned Teddy saying we would be late, mentioning the snow and that we were driving his car. The second half of the journey was grim. Snowstorms and icy twisting mountain roads. I got to the door of the Ski Lodge at 2 A.M. Teddy was hovering anxiously. He came out, walked round the car, examining it carefully, and *then* said, "Darlings, are you all right?" I didn't think it odd. That's how Englishmen *are* about their cars.

Driving in and out of New York City as we frequently do, we have ample opportunity to study the driving manners of Americans. There was a certain amount of terror involved in competing with such enormous vehicles on their own ground. Until I came to America I had met only one Cadillac. This was owned by another neighbor of ours in London. Her parents were a well-known American actor and actress who were very popular in England. When their daughter got married they presented her with a Cadillac, which was kept in what we considered the American way, outside the house. Not that I am suggesting that even an Englishman would keep his car inside the house, but a lock-up garage had to be provided for it or the owner wouldn't sleep o'nights.

The houses were terraced, each house having fifteen feet of frontage on the pavement (sidewalk—American). When the Cadillac arrived it was found to be much longer than the house. The poor girl was in a dilemma. A large piece of car encroached on each of her immediate neighbors' fifteen feet. We are possessive about our pavements when it comes to cars as well as dogs. The young bride tried parking her car with the whole of the excess part in front of her neighbors' houses on alternate days. But her neighbors were always having guests who would have to park too, so finally she had to put it in a public garage where she had to pay the price for parking two cars—small English type.

Having been frightened by this monster—although I never actually tangled with it—I was amazed by the docility of the breed's behavior when I eventually found myself in a large herd of them driving out of New York City. True, they moved at a fast pace, carrying one along with them. But there was no cutting in; all the lines of cars swept into their desired lanes. The only criticism we can make is that one has to know exactly where one has to turn before one takes to the road. There are signs, of course, but because of the speed at which these creatures move, one has often passed the exit one wants by the time one has read the sign. This has caught on to some extent in London where underpasses and overpasses and one-way signs are beginning to hold sway. The last time I drove in London I wanted to go from Knightsbridge to Victoria Station. The obvious way I thought was to drive to Hyde Park Corner—not being clever at finding my way down back streets—and to drive down Grosvenor Place. Imagine my surprise when I found myself driving round Piccadilly Circus with, apparently, no means of escape. After circling it four times I was noticed by a policeman who indicated the route to freedom. I never made Victoria Station. I went home.

One thing one dare not do in England is overtake another car. This *really* brings out the beast in men drivers. Aspersions, they feel, are being cast either on their driving prowess or the performance of their loved one. If by any chance one has been forced by circumstances to pull out and apologetically pass a gentleman driver one must be prepared for the consequences. Whatever the size and horse power of the passed car, however small, one isn't given any peace until he has forced one to pull over to allow him to go by. This he does with a big glare in one's direction. What he never seems to realize is that one hasn't been trying very hard, and that one is delighted to be allowed to tool along at one's own speed and watch his beastly little car disintegrate. This same Britisher would undoubtedly be the most dependable person in the world to have around in times of strife or in disaster —but, my goodness, in his car he's a demon.

While we're on the subject of cars there's one other thing that must be mentioned. Opening car doors for wives. Americans *do* this, I notice. With all the talk about American women being aggressive, in this instance their husbands treat them like frail little flowers. They open the door, see that their wives are tucked in, shut the door securely, then go round to the driver's seat. With most Englishmen one is lucky if one's legs are in before he drives off. Then there are car windows. American husbands will see to it that their wives' hair isn't ruined on the way to a party. The windows are carefully checked for possible drafts. I know, I have observed this many times.

Not so with an Englishman. He might expire on the way to the party if the windows are closed. If it is not actually raining the sliding roof has to be opened. He will offer one his handkerchief to tie over one's head, but everyone knows what a handkerchief will do to one's bouffant hairdo. On arrival the American husband will get out and open the door for his wife. I have seen wives wait for this service and have tried to follow suit, but it didn't work. What's holding you up? I'd be asked.

This seems to be developing into a discussion on the relative merits of American and English husbands. Perhaps the Englishman's attitude to cars is in some ways reflected in his attitude toward his wife. Whatever the reasons, more Englishmen keep their old wives than Americans do. Perhaps he thinks a female he has selected and kept in tune through the years is bound to give him better service in the end. There's a certain sentimental attachment too, and finally, most important of all, the thing they are most proud to advertise. One Owner!

CHAPTER 26

BECAUSE of the various activities connected with Edward's business, most of all the requests he received to make speeches in different parts of the country, the line of demarcation between work and leisure was very hard to define.

We believe a man's work must, of necessity, almost fill his life; but, however interesting the job, it is essential to get away from it at times.

The English businessman in his own country is clever at this. The head of a company will have some other abiding interest, which gets him away from it all. Some interest in which he can lose himself completely and forget for a while that his employees are depending on him for the wherewithal to pay the next installment on the television set or their next trip to Majorca.

In England, the rather grand, possibly fierce, boss will be found pottering around his garden or his farm at weekends, wearing ghastly old clothes which all Englishmen seem to treasure. He'll be building a new pig sty, or digging a drain. This, when he can well afford to employ someone to do it for him. In fact, he undoubtedly does employ people, but the great thing is to wait until they have gone off for the weekend, when he, the boss, can do exactly what he wants to do, in his own way, on his own property. Strange, how often a man whose word is absolute law in a large business concern is frightened of his gardener.

Anyway, with a slight feeling of guilt, which no doubt adds to his pleasure, he immerses himself in a completely different world and returns to his tycoonery on Monday morning with renewed vigor.

In America the weekend does not seem to be sacred to

recharging the batteries. Perhaps this is why so many young-ish men collapse with heart attacks.

In our own lives we found that Teddy's weekends were often taken up with traveling either to get to a place where he had a Monday lunch-time speaking date or with returning home, after a meeting of the minds which would end too late on Friday for him to get back to New York and the bosom of his family. When delays because of weather con-ditions were also taken into account, we found that our week-ends were dwindling away alarmingly. Being in the same hemisphere as my spouse proved to be small comfort, espe-cially when I found on studying a map that the distances separating us were often greater than the distance across the Atlantic to England.

We were all beginning to feel a great desire to melt into the background occasionally. Not easy when one was part of a family which included the "best-known Englishman in America, next to Winston Churchill." So we read, and so we were told, and so Teddy was introduced by countless chair-men across the land.

On hearing this for the first time, I experienced a feeling of panic, which was mitigated by the thought that our own situation would surely change soon. People would get used to the idea of this bearded Englishman landing in their midst, telling them a thing or two, and then departing. It did not improve. Teddy was presently in the public domain, and there seemed to be no getting away from it.

We decided to buy a boat. One in which we could cruise at weekends and seek solitude. This was a long-cherished dream of Teddy's. A sailing boat, of course, but with an aux-iliary engine.

Anyone who has ever decided to buy a boat will know what torments we suffered before it finally arrived. She had been chosen by Edward chiefly for her roominess below decks and the simplicity of her sail plan, which meant that he could handle it alone with my assistance. There were other reasons why he bought it but these are the only two that really concerned me.

I had to be given some initial training, not having had any experience in crewing in anything larger than a 12-sq.-meter Sharpie, a boat in which it is impossible to keep dry.

Our Sharpie had been built for us in England, and was launched a few days before Charles was born. Charles had his first sail in her when he reached the ripe old age of three weeks. For once, Chichester Harbor was blissfully calm, or I'd never have taken him aboard, though very soon he was braving the elements in their different moods in a life jacket, which at first reached his ankles and gradually crept up to his waist, as he grew.

When we decided to prolong our stay in America we had the Sharpie sent from England. It was the year that Sharpies were being raced in the Olympics. The American entry's boat having already been shipped to Australia, the Whitehead Sharpie was used to stretch the American sails and provide the American helmsman with opportunities to continue practice, ours being the only boat of its kind in the country. It might be thought that we could never part with a boat which, for us, had so much history, but I am ashamed to say that when we heard our new cruising boat was about to arrive, we all shut our eyes tightly and presented the Sharpie to the local Sea Scouts.

Ever since, we have had a guilt complex about it as though we had put a child out for adoption, and we are sure we were being repaid for our hardheartedness when the arrival of our new boat was delayed, as it turned out, for a whole season.

When she *did* arrive, I still had to be trained. It was early in the year when we made our first voyage out of Southport harbor, so there were very few boats about. When we got clear of the channel, I was told to take the wheel and keep the boat into the wind while Teddy put up the sails. There was quite a smart little breeze, but I passed my first test, and when Teddy, having hoisted the mainsail, shouted "Bear away" I bore away, though with a slight feeling of alarm because the sail looked so enormous. Once he realized I was not panicking, Teddy got busy, hauling up the jib. This made a big flapping noise which *was* alarming; also, the boat began to heel. My feet were slipping in the cockpit, so I called Teddy to come and take over quickly. He hurriedly made fast the halyards and ran along the deck toward me. As he approached he caught his foot in the framework of the dodger, catapulted into the cockpit, and lay completely still, turning deathly white.

Well, *something* must have got through to me over the years. I realized we were getting into shallow water. I knew I'd have to face a court-martial if I ran aground, so instead of dropping everything and flapping, which I'd have liked to do, I put the wheel over, released the starboard jib-sheet, hauled in on the portside, got it on the winch, belayed it, and tacked out to open water.

I had time to wonder how I'd ever get the boat back into the harbor before Teddy began to stir and look about him with a "where am I?" expression.

For a short while following that episode my status was high, but very soon I found myself relegated to galley duty, in spite of the fact that I always complained that I felt seasick below decks. Which wasn't strictly true.

Alas, our dream of finding solitude was not to be realized. Because of our abbreviated week ends, we had to sail rather close to home. Apart from the fact that we soon discovered the most attractive harbor within our range was the one where we had our own moorings, we also found that what we are forced to think of as American gregariousness applied to the seagoing types as well as to landlubbers.

On one of our early week ends aboard Edward and I sailed across the Sound and found a pleasant place to anchor off a sandy beach. We had a lovely afternoon, swimming off the boat, and, as the weather was set fair, we decided to stay where we were instead of going into a strange harbor and picking up a mooring—one possibly with a view of the local cement works.

We were sitting in the cockpit enjoying the sunset and the solitude when we saw a boat coming toward us. It came very close and the skipper called "Have you a good anchorage there?" "We think so," replied Edward. The boat circled us, then came alongside again. By this time there was another person standing in the bow with a coiled line in his hands, which he threw onto our deck as he got near. "Make this fast," we were ordered. In a slight daze, we made it fast. Was this a boarding party? Were there pirates on Long Island Sound? Did they want to borrow something? We were not told. The crew of the intruder were busying themselves throwing out more lines. One of them came aboard and inspected our knots. Finally, with lines out fore and aft attached to our boat, the skipper said "Great; what about a drink?" We excused ourselves, but we couldn't withdraw—we were only feet away from them.

Edward and I went below decks and in sign language told each other that we thought these people were going to stay the night. We couldn't haul up anchor and sail away, the other boat would have to be unhitched. Still miming, we agreed that we'd have to stay put, but next time anyone asked if we had found a good anchorage we'd tell them we were aground.

Resigned, we crawled back to the cockpit in time to see another boat circling us. A voice was saying "How's the anchorage?" "Fine," said our neighbor, "but you'd better get the other side,"—on *our* side, he meant. Once again we were boarded. Lines were made fast to our cleats. We were told to let them out, haul them in, make them fast. Once again we obeyed. We were numb. Our hopes of an evening swim were shattered. We couldn't go down our ladder without danger of being squashed.

By this time Skipper No. 1, a jolly type, had invited Skipper No. 2 and his ship's complement to join him for drinks.

This Skipper No. 2 did, by crossing our boat, accompanied by a throng of people wearing what sounded from the cabin like hobnailed boots, or possibly, as there were ladies among them, spike heels.

Edward and I now realized we were trapped. Whether we joined the party or not we were going to be very much in the center of it. Wearing forced smiles we went up on deck and joined the merry group.

The inevitable happened. There were glad cries of "You *are* Commander Whitehead, aren't you?" The party continued. The laughter became more raucous.

Teddy was determined to stay to the bitter end and to ensure that everyone took off their shoes when recrossing his decks, but we had to retire, defeated.

Back in our own boat, we had to undress in the dark to avoid being observed through the portholes. *I* felt we were too close to the other boats to use the head, but Teddy had no such inhibitions.

Neither had the other people. When finally the party broke up I lay in my little bunk and heard the bathroom pumpings of eight people. All strangers.

I suppose the stars came out that night. The soft wind blew over the sea and the tide lapped round the boat. Perhaps fish jumped in the darkness. We don't know. We were stuck between two boats in each of which someone was snoring.

The worst of it was (and all sailors, and some motor boat people will understand this) they were both motor cruisers.

The complete antithesis of this adventure is the story of a short cruise undertaken by some friends of ours in England.

They had sailed across the Solent to the Isle of Wight to a certain cove which they regarded as their own. Hoping to avoid the possibility of sharing it with any one else, they cruised mid-week on this occasion instead of at the week end.

The weather was glorious; June in England can be perfect. Our friend, who is a doctor, his wife, and their son and daughter were on board. They had a blissful evening swimming, fishing, and there was utter silence.

Next morning they woke early to enjoy the beautiful day. The doctor and his son got into the dinghy to row ashore and get fresh milk from a farm for the morning tea. As they left, the wife put the kettle on the stove in the galley so that the water would be boiling by the time her husband returned. The daughter was on deck soaking up the early sunshine when she saw another boat sail into their cove. A boat she recognized. Although disappointed that they would no longer be able to enjoy the heavenly morning alone, she called her mother, who was below, to come and wave at the invaders. The mother stood at the top of the companionway trying to look welcoming. At that moment there was the dull *whoomph* of an explosion. The mother was flung into the water, the daughter jumped in after her, the father and son now close to shore turned round to see their beautiful boat sinking.

The second boat was owned and being sailed by our old friend Nevil Shute (now, alas, dead), and it was he who told us the story.

When he sailed into the cove and found it already occupied he was disappointed too, and would have sailed out immediately had he not recognized the moored boat. He thought he'd better do the polite thing and sail by to say good morning before he retreated. He was fairly close when he heard the explosion, and saw what he thought was a bundle of rags describe an arc into the water. The doctor's wife in her dressing gown, a nonswimmer. He was able to pick her and the daughter out of the water in the three minutes it took for the stricken yacht to disappear into the translucent water. However, he said, when they got round to discussing the event, he couldn't be sure that they weren't more cross with him for finding their cove than they were grateful to him for being there at the right time.

The British are sometimes gregarious but usually they

yearn for some quiet spot where they can relax in peace. The old cliché, "An Englishman's home is his castle," is as true today as it was when it was first uttered. His garden is also his castle, and he surrounds it with fences and hedges and walls, so that he *can* only be attacked via the front door. This way he can be at home, or not at home, to unexpected visitors as *he* pleases.

I remember looking at a house with a friend in England. There was another house fairly close, but separated by an impenetrable yew hedge. My friend peered out of every window in turn and all she could see was a lovely garden and trees until she got to the upstairs "loo," a tiny room with a narrow window about five feet from the floor. She climbed onto the "loo," opened the window, and craned her neck out. She could see part of the roof of the other house and about one third of a dormer window. "Too bad," she said, "we'd be overlooked."

Having these feelings deep in our souls we find it difficult to understand the American custom of fenceless gardens. After all, it was an American poet who said "Good fences make good neighbors." I like to walk about in our garden in the early morning in my nightgown, but only if I am sure I am going to be alone and unobserved.

In terms of privacy, cruising in our boat turned out to be a snare and a delusion.

The actual sailing was lovely. It really was bliss to sail about under a sunny sky with enough breeze to make the boat go well without scaring the wits out of me. There were days when the winds were really strong, when the Sound changed its character completely, and we scudded about with the lee rail awash (if you know what I mean). Fortunately, when this happened there was usually someone else on board other than myself to obey the commands issued by Teddy. Commands to "free that genoa up forrard," or "make fast that anchor, or halyard" or "belay that spinnaker sheet"—commands which usually involved creeping to the front end of the boat, with spray dashing over one and an extremely lop-sided view of the horizon; commands that I found remarkably uninspiring. But our real problems began when we were stationary. In a dead calm we would anchor so that we could swim. I always get into the water by going down the ladder, but Teddy would dive off the bow. As he stood there poised for flight, a boat would pass by; there'd be a double take on the part of the occupants, and the boat (they were usually small, easily maneuverable craft) would begin circling us. Teddy would dive in, and strike off in determined fashion toward England. As he always wears earplugs when swimming he'd be completely cut off from the ensuing conversation.

"Is that the guy in the Schweppes ads?"

"Glub." I am not very loquacious in the water.

"Is his name really *Commander* Whitehead?"

"Glub." (Of course!)

"Is this his boat?"

"Glub." (Naturally.)

"Are you Mrs. Whitehead?"

"Glub." (Who else?)

"Do you think he'd give us an autograph?"

"Glub, glub." (angrily).

"How far is he going to swim?"

"Glub—Help—" this as I became aware that I had strayed too far from the ladder.

When we had to tie up to an alien dock, there'd be similar problems.

To stroll about on a quay or dock and look at the boats is a fascinating occupation. One in which we have indulged as much as anyone. But never would we sit on the edge of the dock studying a boat when the owners were aboard.

We began to feel like bears in a bearpit; we almost expected the audience to throw buns.

I shudder to think of how many snapshots there must be in existence of Edward climbing out of the hatchway of his boat and looking slightly indignant as he spied a camera focused on him. I don't really shudder about that, of course, because Edward can hold his own with any amateur photographer, sheltered as he is behind his beard. The shudders arrive when I think of the number of times I have inadvertently been included in the snapshots, before having a chance to brush my hair or put on my eye black; looking like a rat peering out of a ball of oakum.

I can hear it now—"What's this little animal?"

"It's Mrs. Whitehead."

"My God—"

CHAPTER 27

AFTER a decade in the United States the outstanding fact is that no one we have met has criticized Britain to us. I am excluding the man at the cocktail party who didn't care for British sex. And the taxi driver who, while driving me from the airport, told me that Britain was battening on the United States; that the United States was always leaping into the fray to help Britain with her wars. His reflected baleful eye was fixed on me while I nervously reminded him of Pearl Harbor. He brushed that off and went on to castigate all European countries, as well as the Republican and Democratic parties in the United States, the Queen of England, and Russia; there was *nothing* he loved, except the fact that he had a trapped audience. He was really beastly about everything; but even he, no doubt feeling better having got so much hate off his chest, said "It sure has been nice talking with you" when I thankfully left him.

We have, of course, had give-and-take discussions about the United States and Britain with people who know both countries well, but the thousands of ordinary Americans we have met, who have never been to Britain, are the ones whose generous attitude has impressed us. Perhaps this is the best example of American good manners. The people we were meeting knew we were British so, whatever their secret thoughts, they expressed interest in and a desire to know more about our country and always seemed proud to tell us of some remote connection with the British Isles.

We have to admit, sometimes, to feeling a tiny bit ashamed of our own countrymen when they criticize Americans and the American way of life without ever having visited the United States.

Our sentiments could not be better expressed than by the following excerpt from a letter our son sent us about four weeks after he had been at his school in English, where he is now perfectly happy and beginning to perceive the advantages of living and being educated on both sides of the Atlantic. It may be remembered that at his American school he had had to defend the British in small ways. Now, at his English school, he found the position reversed. He wrote, "I have made many friends and assorted enemies. The enemies are boys who make cracks about America and I make it my business to enlighten them."

Perhaps the silliest question we have been asked, on both sides of the Atlantic, is "Which country do you like best?" If, after ten years, America does not feel like home to us, there is something wrong *with us*. But England is still home too.

We feel annoyed, hurt, and defensive when we read what we consider to be unfair criticism of Britain in the American press. By the same token we get mad, upset, and again defensive when we read articles in British newspapers castigating America. We are like children of separated parents, both of whom we love. We owe loyalty to both and cannot bear to hear one criticize the other.

The cross section of American people we have met has included the rich, the poor, the educated, the illiterate. The beautiful and handsome, the fat and ugly, and the plain ordinary. Snobs (they *do* exist in America), intellectuals, bores, wits, Negroes, Japanese. Sad people, happy ones, go-getters and the lazy (though not many of these. In America they really do work for their rewards). Horrid old ladies with loud voices and beautiful gentle ones who tend their gardens in summer and love cats. Sweet old boys with an eye for the girls and annoyingly persistent wolves. Young men with an urge to do something toward making the world a better place to live in, and beatniks who don't want to do anything and can't. Disciplined children, spoiled brats, women who are frustrated by the confines of their lives and husbands who feel guilty because they feel they might be responsible. Flouters of convention, puritanical squares, insensitive clods, and many people we are proud to think of as friends.

For every one of these people—and there are many more categories—we could find a counterpart among our friends and acquaintances in the British Isles. With the exception of the Japanese. We don't know any Japanese in England.

The longer we live in America, the more the gap narrows. Either England is becoming Americanized—a thing that, oddly enough, Americans have *complained* about to us—or America, having boisterously grown into a front-rank nation in such a short space of time, is now settling down and developing some of the traits of the former leaders of the world. Goodness, they even have tea bags and sliced bread—revolting stuff—in England now, and recently I heard a man, an American, ask for his beer to be left out of the icebox to get warm before he drank it.

Among other things, Edward has had to defend, or not, according to his own opinions, the British position during the Suez crisis, trading with Red China, our omission to follow the lead of the early invaders from Rome in the matter of central heating, British aloofness, plumbing, and recently, moral turpitude. English women, food, socialized medicine, and cricket. Selling buses to Cuba, and the climate (every taxi driver asks how do the British survive in all that fog. I now retaliate by telling them how I nearly went blind in Los Angeles). Finally, sensationalism in the press, the attitude of some British pressmen, and biased reporting.

Some of the American things he has had to defend in England are the American way of life, cars, women, central heating, sensationalism in the press, and biased reporting. To Edward whose career has depended on his interest in diverse subjects and who has no difficulty at all in stringing words together, it is second nature to expound on any given subject.

In my twelve years in America I have also held forth at

times, much to my own surprise. I have fallen in love with certain things and some of them have become part of my life. In case I haven't mentioned them before, here are a few of them:

Contemporary architecture
Colonial houses
The George Washington Bridge at night
Ed. Murrow
Sardi's
Vermont
The Guggenheim
Hollywood beds—and
The Tonight Show, when I am alone in one
New York on a clear night
Jazz
Men's voices on the telephone
Skating ponds in winter
Swimming in warm water
Snowy Christmases
Leonard Bernstein
Tugboats on the East River
Ice floes on the Hudson
Central heating that works
Humming birds
Pequot Yacht Club
Aspetuck
Channel 13
Johnny Seesaws
Old New England churches
Phoebes
Stowehof
Ground hogs
Fireflies
Corn-on-the-cob
Erling Ström

Blueberry pie (Whitehead version)
Catbirds
Patty Gagarin's ski clothes
Dr. John Eckel
Enough bathrooms
Shopping for clothes
New York taxi drivers (but only if their cabs are clean and
    they don't spit out the window)
Paper towels
Below zero
Café Nicholson
Danny Kaye
Clam chowder
The Lincoln Center
The *New Yorker*
Apple barns
The telephone service
The Merritt Parkway in spring
Parke Bernet
The Metropolitan Opera House
The picture galleries
Modern ballet
Short Skis

A simple enough list, but, to plagiarize, mine own.

An equally long list could be made of the things that mean
Britain to us, things we miss all the time.

In whichever direction we happen to be crossing the
Atlantic we now feel, "Hooray we're going home."

We land in England and we're met by Jacq and Keith.
There is a slight feeling of strangeness because people are
never quite as one remembers them. We pick up Charles
from school and go to the Cottage where the children are
waiting. We change into cottage clothes and walk in a solid
phalanx round the sea wall. Within five minutes we feel we

have never been away. That we are back in the past before Sarah and Jason and Jasper were born, though now it is impossible to imagine the Cottage without them.

At night we jump into our old familiar bed. The pillows "go" exactly right. We are lulled to sleep by the hooting of owls and the sound of the wind blowing in the branches of the ancient yews. America is a long long way away.

When we come back to America, we are sad to leave our family but as we approach New York we find ourselves getting excited. Poody, our American cat, doomed by English laws never to see the Cottage, is waiting for us. Things have happened in the garden in Connecticut. The lilies, which we thought would never survive the winter and the chipmunks, are in full bloom against the old stone wall.

We jump into our familiar bed and the pillows feel just right. We are lulled to sleep by the chirping of crickets. We're back home—and England is a long long way away.

I SEEM to have written an awful lot about my own feelings as the wife of a man who found himself not only in the public eye but almost in the public grasp. But what about Edward? There cannot ever have been a man less changed by his situation.

His energy and enthusiasm are legendary as well as his kindness. Perhaps this is what shines through and makes it possible for all sorts of people to approach him for autographs or just to talk. He feels it would be unnecessarily cruel to brush off a meek little person who accosts him with an apologetic smile. But loud voiced back-slappers make him freeze and they are apt to get a stony stare.

Sometimes the thought is voiced that without the original concept, putting Edward in the advertising, the business might not have prospered as it did, but what is genius but making the most of opportunities as they arise, and in his case turning an unwelcome situation to good account. Anyway, I know Teddy—with him, something good always happens. Apart from the excitement of building up a business, the thing that has really made Edward feel he can bear his goldfish-bowl existence is the inner satisfaction he gets from being a sort of unofficial ambassador for Britain. Up and down the country, from East to West, he has done so much more than beat the bushes for business.

But what now? Although out of Edward's busy year only a week to ten days is devoted to actual commercials or photography, he feels restive. "Just this once" has become twelve years. Will it go on, even unto the second generation?

Son of Schweppesman, perhaps?

Heaven forfend!